TO PATRICK CALLEO

The German Problem Reconsidered

It is characteristic of the Germans that the question:
"What is German?" never dies out among them.
Friedrich Nietzsche, Beyond Good and Evil

The German Problem Reconsidered

Germany and the World Order, 1870 to the Present

DAVID CALLEO
Professor of European Studies
Director of the European Studies Program
The Johns Hopkins School of Advanced International Studies

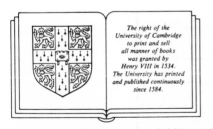

*The right of the
University of Cambridge
to print and sell
all manner of books
was granted by
Henry VIII in 1534.
The University has printed
and published continuously
since 1584.*

CAMBRIDGE UNIVERSITY PRESS

Cambridge
New York   Port Chester
Melbourne   Sydney

Published by the Press Syndicate of the University of Cambridge
The Pitt Building, Trumpington Street, Cambridge CB2 1RP
40 West 20th Street, New York, NY 10011, USA
10 Stamford Road, Oakleigh, Melbourne 3166, Australia

First published 1978
First paperback edition 1980
Reprinted 1982, 1984, 1986, 1988, 1990

Printed in the United States of America

Library of Congress Cataloging in Publication Data
Calleo, David P, 1934–
The German problem reconsidered.
Bibliography: p.
1. Germany – History – 1871–1918. 2. Germany –
History – 20th century. 3. World politics –
19th century. 4. World politics – 20th century.
5. Germany – History – Philosophy. 1. Title.
DD220.C34 943.08 78–9683

ISBN 0-521-22309-1 hardback
ISBN 0-521-29966-7 paperback

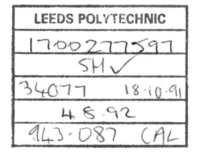

Contents

Preface

This book, whatever its shortcomings, has benefited greatly from the assistance of others. If good advice has not always been taken, it has always been freely given. Thanks to The Lehrman Institute in New York, the chapters have been presented in draft form before a seminar of historians and other German experts. Many of the participants have been kind enough to write detailed commentaries. In particular, I should like to thank Hans Gatzke, Peter Katzenstein, Fritz Stern, and Henry Turner, as well as my old friends and colleagues at the Institute, Harold van Buren Cleveland, Robert Heilbroner, Lewis Lehrman, and Nicholas Rizopoulos.

Kendall Myers, Edward Keeton, and Robert Skidelsky, colleagues and former colleagues at the Johns Hopkins School of Advanced International Studies, have been no less generous. I am particularly grateful to Stephen Schuker, of Brandeis University and S.A.I.S., for his advice on the manuscript's final version. A long list of students and research assistants have made major contributions, in particular Jacqueline Tammenoms-Bakker, Jordan Barab,

John Berger, Andreas Credé, David Haettenschwiller, John Harper, Marnix Krop, Eric Melby, and Prescott Wurlitzer. The dissertations of four of my students — Robert Dahlberg, Simon Newman, Francis Rome, and Benjamin Rowland — have greatly contributed to the further education of their professor and to this book in particular.

Another important source of advice and criticism has been two distinguished German scholars at the University of Cologne, Hans-Peter Schwarz and Andreas Hillgruber. Both read the manuscript in an early draft and went out of their way to make numerous helpful comments. My thanks, too, for the good advice of my friends Wolfram Hanrieder, Eckehard Loerke, and Joan Cleveland.

My researches in Germany have been greatly helped by the hospitality of Professor Kurt Sontheimer at the Geschwister-Scholl-Institut at the University of Munich, and that of Karl Kaiser and Wolfgang Hager at the Forschungsinstitut für Auswärtige Politik in Bonn. Interviews with German businessmen, civil servants, journalists, politicians, and scholars, too numerous to mention, have been indispensable in helping me understand the contemporary German economic and political situation. I thank all those busy people for their kind and patient help. For the time and funds for these researches, I can thank the Johns Hopkins University, the Fulbright Commission, and my friend, Lewis Lehrman.

For the usual vast labors of typing and checking drafts, I thank my student assistants, and, in particular, Jordan Barab, who prepared the index, also my secretary, Winifred Williams, and the secretaries at the Lehrman Institute, Betty Gurchick, Dida Porecki, and Carol Rath. For her usual careful editing and advice, my thanks also to May Wu at the Lehrman Institute.

Finally, despite this rather gregarious process, writing a book is a lonely and exasperating affair. For providing so warm a home for me in Germany, and for their innumerable insights into the country and its people, I thank my brother, Patrick, and his wife, Lynn. To these brief personal acknowledgments, I must add the support and forbearance of my wife, Avis.

D. C.

1

Introduction: The German Problem and its Significance

To a remarkable extent, world history from the 1860s to after the Second World War has been dominated by the German Problem. What is, or was, that problem? Its international aspect can most easily be summarized by a question: Why, since the 1860s, has Germany been so often at war with its neighbors? There is a domestic aspect as well: What made a Nazi regime possible in so advanced and civilized a country?

Like the German Problem itself, the theories that explain it have their international and domestic components. Internationally, a united Germany is often said to have been too big and dynamic for any stable European state system. Inevitably, such a Germany threatened the political independence and economic well-being of its neighbors. Germany's dynamic expansiveness, in turn, is frequently said to have stemmed from the internal character of the German nation — the political institutions, culture, and economic and social systems that evolved during the nineteenth and twentieth centuries. This character is thought not only to have made Germany uncommonly

aggressive abroad, but also particularly susceptible to totalitarianism at home.

For many people, these theories lead to a single practical
conclusion: Whenever unified into one state, Germans
become a menace at home and abroad. And this conclusion, shared by the postwar leaderships of all Germany's
neighbors, leads to an obvious prescription: To keep
Europe safe, and the German people safe from themselves,
Germany must be firmly contained by alert and superior
power. Had the lesson only been learned and applied earlier, it is frequently said, the world would have been spared
at least the second of this century's general wars. By similar
reasoning, the postwar Russian American duopoly over
Europe is now thought to have resolved the German Problem.

Behind such attitudes lies a vast body of analytical writing that ascribes the German Problem primarily to the
international policies of the Germans themselves and
traces those policies to the inner compulsions of German
society. Much of this writing is distinguished and full of
insight. Understandably, most of it is infused with an intense
reaction against war in general and Nazi racial policy in
particular. As time goes by, however, a good deal of this
analysis seems unbalanced – vulnerable to two major criti-
cisms. First of all, Germany is too often treated as an isolated case, a country with broad characteristics presumed
not to exist elsewhere. Many German writers appear to take
a certain perverse relish in claiming for their society a
unique wickedness among humankind. Obviously, every
national society is in many senses unique. And although no
one should wish to rob the Germans of their hard-earned
reputation, theirs is not the only European society with, for
example, closely knit families, an emphasis on private
rather than public virtues, or authoritarian traditions. Nor
is Germany the only nation that has hoped to play a great
role in bringing the world to order or taken pride in mili-

tary prowess. Nor indeed have such traits and ambitions been conspicuously absent from the international arena since Germany's defeat in 1945. Particularly questionable is the widespread view that the Germans were uniquely afflicted with nineteenth-century Romanticism and Philosophical Idealism. It should not be so easy for cultural historians to forget the influence of Bergson in France, nor of the Romantics and Philosophical Idealists in Britain.

Secondly, this habit of seeing German culture as unique has a parallel in the tendency to view German unification as a malevolent accident that befell an otherwise harmonious European system. From a broader perspective, however, Germany's consolidation and the conflicts that ensued were only the natural consequences of Europe's evolution into national states. From the Middle Ages, the European peoples had tried a variety of imperial and federal forms. By the nineteenth century, the nation-state increasingly seemed the only effective political formula for organizing stable government over modern societies. Limiting states to national units obviously carried with it the problem of an "international" system. Because the national states coexisted so closely in Europe, they were inevitably preoccupied with the "balance" among them. By the end of the nineteenth century, moreover, they had reached out to bring most of the globe within their political-economic orbit. This outward expansion had incalculable consequences. It profoundly altered Europe's internal relationships. And it created or awakened powerful new forces from beyond Europe, first the rising semi-European giants – Russia and the United States, later Japan, and, in our own day, the "Third World."

The German Problem ought properly to be seen within the context of this broad evolution of the Western national states and the international issues which that evolution inevitably posed. Germany was the last of the great European national states to be formed. The Germans had paid a heavy price for their historic procrastination. It was not comfortable to be only a loose federation surrounded by centralized nation-states. Indeed, throughout most of modern history, Germans were more often victims than aggressors. Hideously ravaged by invaders in the Thirty Years' War, the German territories became a sort of athletic field for playing out the various dynastic ambitions of the ancien régime. Later, the French Revolution brought some two decades of invasion and occupation. A good part of the Germans' ill fortune came from having failed to consolidate a national state before their neighbors. The first great unifying attempt, launched by the Holy Roman Emperor Ferdinand II during the Thirty Years' War, had been finally abandoned by 1648. Many factors were at work in the defeat, religious divisions, jealousy and greed among the German princes. But above all the prospects for German union were destroyed from without. The German national effort became caught up in Bourbon France's struggle with Habsburg Spain. Thus, the French Cardinals Richelieu and Mazarin, in alliance with Protestant Swedes, infidel Turks, and Pope Urban VIII, defeated Catholic Habsburg power in Germany. With Germany devastated and disunited, the European scene was dominated for 200 years by the rivalry of France and Britain.

Not until after the Napoleonic invasions did the Germans turn away from their cosmopolitan and particularist tradition and begin to adopt the unifying nationalism of their neighbors. Once a national state was achieved, there was no reason to assume that a powerful new Germany would prove any less expansive than France, which had continually sought to dominate Europe, or Britain, which had conquered an enormous world empire. Germany's economic growth, moreover, was extremely rapid. By 1900, the new Reich had not only overshadowed France on the Continent, but its economic power had penetrated deep into Russia and was competing successfully with Britain throughout the world. Under the circumstances, dynamic Germany was found to appear an aggressor, challenging the arrangements that had grown up in its absence and that presumed its continuing weakness. Germany was driven not only by the desire to overtake a declining Britain, but also by the fear of being overshadowed by a rising Russia and United States. In the race for the future, Germans saw themselves already fatally handicapped. For while the United States, Russia, and even Britain were on the periphery of Europe, Germany lay in its middle. Whereas the growth of superpowers on the Eastern or Western edges only indirectly undermined the European status quo, German ambitions assaulted it directly. Hence, while Britain came to preside over half the globe, and both Russia and the United States relentlessly filled out their continental hinterlands, Germany was expected to remain locked within the tight frame of Europe's traditional balance of power. From a German view, preserving the European balance, while extra-European giants formed all around, meant condemning Germany to mediocrity and, ultimately, all of Europe to external domination. That was the German Problem as the Germans saw it.

To analyze Germany's ambitions and fears as essentially the product of its own unusual political culture subtly distorts history in favor of Germany's victors. For Britain, France, Russia, and the United States were great powers with appetites no less ravenous than Germany's. The desire to control foreign space and resources – the preoccupation with room for growth – went hand in hand with modernization in nearly all major countries. Indeed it is one of the more remarkable accomplishments of modern historiography that the Germans, who never had a serious formal empire, should come to be seen as the most virulent carriers of the imperialist disease. In short, Germany's "aggressiveness" against international order may be explained as plausibly by the nature of that order as by any

peculiar characteristics of the Germans. Even Germany's
Nazi episode may be seen less as the consequence of some
inherent flaw in German civilization, some autonomous
national cancer developing according to its own inner
rhythm, than of the intense pressures put upon Germany
from the outside. Geography and history conspired to
make Germany's rise late, rapid, vulnerable, and aggressive. The rest of the world reacted by crushing the upstart.
If, in the process, the German state lost its bearings and
was possessed by an evil demon, perhaps the proper conclusion is not so much that civilization was uniquely weak
in Germany, but that it is fragile everywhere. And perhaps
the proper lesson is not so much the need for vigilance
against aggressors, but the ruinous consequences of refusing reasonable accommodation to upstarts.

No doubt it is the privilege of victors to write history in
their favor. Nevertheless, as the Second World War grows
further away in time, and as we grow less confident of our
own virtue, wisdom, and power, or of the system that our
victory imposed upon the world, perhaps we are ready to
consider the German Problem in a new light. In particular,
we might consider the major alternatives for the Western
state system that were bound up with Germany's ambitions.

Does considering these alternatives have any practical
significance? Today, the German drama has seemingly
played itself out. Defeated Germany is once again disunited. The world's two superpowers, each ascendant over
its half of Europe, together prevent reunification. Thus,
the postwar settlement is supposed to have eliminated the
traditional German Problem. Many signs, moreover, suggest a long duration for that settlement. Fear of nuclear
war stabilizes relations between the superpowers. Russian
might appears to guarantee Soviet domination over Eastern
Europe, and "interdependence" seems to confirm American ascendancy in the West. The rising Third World may
well increase Europe's dependence even further. Above all,

the two German states, with their impressive economic revivals, appear resigned – indeed contented – with Germany's national fate. Thus, the German Problem is thought to have passed into history. The force that provoked two world wars has finally been contained. Nowadays, the serious problems of international order lie, it is said, between the superpowers, or "North" and "South," rather than among the advanced capitalist countries themselves.

Old issues, however, sometimes reappear in new guises. Just as we cannot understand the present without knowing the past, so we cannot really understand the past without glimpsing the future. And, as we contemplate the future, it cannot be taken for granted that the present condition of Germany, or of Europe, is eternal. Germany may not be content to stay divided forever; Europe may not be happy to remain locked in an American–Soviet condominium. Indeed, in our mounting troubles with the Common Market, we may find the "German" Problem transformed into the "European" Problem – an appropriately Hegelian revenge upon the Anglo-Saxon victors.

The essays that follow examine various past and present aspects of the German Problem in the light of this broader perspective. Such a work inevitably must leave out a good deal as well as make liberal use of the insights of others. I do not claim to produce new scholarship on the many topics that are discussed, but rather to look at old scholarship in a new frame. In many instances, I do not attempt to offer new interpretations, but only to point out the shortcomings of the old ones. It is my hope both to encourage a more balanced understanding of Germany's role in modern history, one at least less obviously tailored to fit the postwar status quo, and also to suggest the continuing relevance of the traditional issues of modern Western history. World history neither began nor ended in 1945. It would not stop for Hegel's Prussian state; it is not likely to stop for our Pax Americana.

2

The Rise of the German Problem: Bismarck's Foreign Policy

Upstart Germany

Once Bismarck had put together the German Empire, his principal diplomatic achievement lay in postponing its confrontation with the rest of Europe. By defeating Austria and France while unifying Germany under Prussia, Bismarck could not help but profoundly challenge the European balance of power. A coalition of hostile powers was nearly inevitable, and indeed appeared as early as 1875, when Britain and Russia both made clear they would not tolerate another German victory over France. Hence, that "nightmare of coalitions," which haunted Bismarck and ultimately did destroy the Reich that he had created. But while Bismarck led Germany, the nightmare never took substance. Can it therefore be said that Bismarck had a foreign policy which, if continued, would have preserved his Reich, a policy his successors were too ambitious or inept to continue?

Bismarck's Defensive Alliances

Essentially, Bismarck's celebrated foreign policy consisted of a complex set of agreements meant to keep all the other powers perpetually off balance. Austria, Italy, and Russia were embraced in German alliances, thus denying their support to French plans for revenge and containing their own rivalries with each other. The rivalry of Russia and Austria-Hungary was to be contained by their mutual alliance with Germany, the Dreikaiserbund, while the tensions between Italy and Austria-Hungary were to be controlled by Germany within the Triple Alliance. Meanwhile, the French were encouraged in those colonial ambitions that guaranteed friction with Britain and Italy. Finally, Bismarck sought to maneuver the British into a certain dependence by encouraging them to guarantee Turkey against Russia and France. Russia, thus restrained in Eastern Europe by Germany's diplomatic embrace, and in the Near East by Britain's Turkish guarantee, was supposed to expand further in Asia, where conflict with Britain and its later ally, Japan, became probable. Britain, thus menaced by the extra-European ambitions of both France and Russia, was expected to look to Germany for support. As a result of all these complex constructions, Germany was to be Europe's diplomatic arbiter. Conflict would be directed away from Europe so as not to disturb its local equilibrium and force Germany into dangerous choices.

Bismarck's alliance policy, it is often said, worked as long as the old virtuoso was in charge. But in the hands of clumsy successors, it soon went awry. Russia was allowed to escape the German embrace when Bismarck's successor as chancellor, Caprivi, foolishly allowed the Russian Reinsurance Treaty to lapse in 1890. Russia began to wander and within a few years allied with Paris. France's isolation was ended and the anti-German coalition Bismarck had feared began to gather. Britain, it is argued, was pushed into the anti-German camp by the ineptitude of German diplomacy, given over to William II's diffuse colonial and naval expansionism and even more undisciplined language. Britain began to see Germany as a greater threat than its traditional rivals, France and Russia. With Britain thus estranged, the attempt to hold Italy within the Triple Alliance, and thus to contain Austrian and Italian rivalry, grew increasingly unreal. As a result, in less than a quarter century after Bismarck's fall, his upstart Reich, supported only by a tottering Austria-Hungary, was left exposed to the combined hostility of Europe's other Great Powers.

Although this familiar argument obviously explains a great deal, it exaggerates Bismarck's personal significance and ignores other fundamental forces at play. Whereas Bülow, Bethmann-Hollweg, or the kaiser lacked Bismarck's diplomatic mastery, a policy that could only be sustained by the ceaseless exertions of shifty genius was unsound and very probably doomed to collapse. The Bismarckian alliance system was, in fact, seriously undermined by the time Bismarck departed. Success depended not only upon Germany's remaining the balancing partner in so many awkward triangles, but also upon convincing the rest of the world that Germany was a sated power. After 1870, such may well have been Bismarck's own view of Germany's interest. He firmly suppressed the dream of completing national union by absorbing Habsburg Germany and he generally tried his best to dampen German colonial ambitions. Renunciation of further expansion had many attractions for Bismarck, determined as he seems to have been to maintain Prussia's authoritarian monarchy and its domination over Germany. Both Prussia's kind of monarchy and its hegemony would be threatened in a Reich that included all the German states, let alone contiguous alien populations. A Germany formed with Austria would swallow Prussia and its traditions and very likely be ungovernable. Moreover, such a Big Germany would surely drive the rest of Europe to react. Hence Bismarck's restraint after defeating Austria in 1866 and his subsequent effort to keep the Dual Monarchy viable.

But whatever Bismarck's own preferences, his Reich was not likely to remain a satisfied power in the world that was evolving after 1870. First of all, there was the dynamic force of nationalism itself. Bismarck began as Cavour and ended as Metternich. He had had to summon German nationalism to consolidate his Reich. He was then through with redrawing the map of Europe. But nationalism was a powerful and wayward force, not easily "fine tuned" to fit the exigencies of power politics. The nationalist wave that created first Italy and then Germany was unlikely to stop short of the Balkans and Poland. Neither Slavs nor Germans were likely to remain contented indefinitely with the status quo in Central and Eastern Europe. The Habsburg monarchy, already defeated by Piedmont and Prussia, would predictably face new challenges that might well exceed its strength. Bismarck's Reich could not remain indifferent to the fate of so many traditional German regions and interests. Nor could it, without ceasing to be a Great Power, permit Russia to dominate the Balkans. Thus, future German governments would almost inevitably be drawn into Eastern territorial disputes.

As it happened, nationalist expansionism was powerfully reinforced by economic considerations. The Great Depression, which stretched from the early 1870s to the late 1890s, significantly affected not only domestic politics but also relations among states. With widespread bankruptcy and prolonged unemployment, governments were constrained from free trade toward protectionism, economic blocs, and imperialism. Bismarck's celebrated shift in domestic policy in 1878 was part of this pattern. His subsequent changes in foreign policy, in particular the "organic" dual alliance with Austria-Hungary, seem to fit as well. In any event, protectionism made his original "satisfied" foreign policy increasingly unrealistic.

Bismarck's Political Economy

In the early years of the Reich, Bismarck's domestic policy was in a Liberal and free-trade phase that harmonized easily with his "satisfied" foreign policy. He courted his erstwhile parliamentary enemies, the National Liberals — upper-middle-class nationalists closely tied to industry and the universities. The Liberals could not help but be grateful for Bismarck's having given Germany a national state. He played skillfully upon their national feeling by his continual alarms against the Reich's presumed enemies at home, like the Catholics, or abroad, like the French. Bismarck also pleased the Liberals by encouraging the rapid growth of commerce and industry and following a general policy of free trade. Free trade and laissez-faire went hand in hand not only with his domestic alliance with the Liberals, but also with his peaceful, "satiated" foreign policy. A free-trade world system would provide outlets for the burgeoning industry and commerce that laissez-faire fostered at home. As long as free trade prevailed, more territory in Europe, or colonies beyond, seemed unnecessary for Germany's political and economic fulfillment.

With the onset of the Great Depression in 1873, the political and economic foundations of Bismarck's domestic and foreign policy began to give way. German heavy industry, the crucial iron and steel industries in particular, had overextended in the boom of the late sixties and early seventies. As the world depression wore on, big industry, in Germany as elsewhere, turned to concentration, cartels, and protectionism.

Protectionism was a way of adjustment to the depression. It involved not merely tariffs, but a general restructuring of industry. Firms were sharply reduced in number and integrated vertically. Home markets were cartelized. Secured by tariffs at home, German firms could dump their "surplus" production abroad at highly competitive prices. Of the major countries, only Britain resisted this pattern, at least in part. Although the Germans were probably no more tied to protection than others, they seemed exceptionally efficient at exploiting its advantages. Thus, despite the prolonged depression, Germany's iron and steel industry grew until it dominated international markets and far surpassed in size that of all other countries, except the equally protectionist United States.

While German private business took the lead in this revolutionary restructuring, Bismarck's state came to play an important role in facilitating it. The necessary tariffs, trade treaties, and company laws were forthcoming. Bismarck was far from ignorant or uninterested in business matters. Germany's government and bureaucracy were open and sensitive to business interests. Business influence was well represented in the Reichstag, and various industrial and trade associations grew into powerful pressure groups, involved increasingly in shaping and mobilizing public opinion through the press and various mass organizations. In short, the Bismarckian state could not, and certainly did not, stand apart either from the transformation of the German economy or from the pursuit of its economic interests abroad.

The state grew further involved as big agriculture also began demanding protection from imports. By the 1880s, as Russia and the United States developed modern transportation systems, their exports increasingly threatened German grain farming, traditional preserve of the Prussian Junkers. Thus, the big Junker agrarians gradually shifted to the protectionist camp. Their political weight was formidable. Bismarck, after all, was himself a big landowner from this class. Junker agrarians controlled the powerful

Agrarian League, which mobilized farming interests. And they were mainstays of the Conservative party. Through it, they controlled the Prussian Landtag, whose election procedures were weighted in their favor.

In addition to the demands of heavy industry and big agriculture, the government faced another major problem exacerbated by the depression. The new Reich was gradually transformed from a land of stable farms and villages into a volatile industrial society. Giant industry meant mass labor, not easily controlled by traditional patriarchal discipline. The depression sharpened labor's discontent, and helped feed the rapid growth of the Social Democratic party. Possessing classes grew nervous at its rising militancy and strength.

By the mid-1870s, as the depression and its attendant dissatisfactions refused to go away, Bismarck realized the need for a new combination of policies and forces. By 1878, he was abandoning his domestic liberalism for a policy that combined protectionism for industry and agriculture with social welfare for workers. In the process, he split the old free-trade National Liberal party, ostracized its progressive wing, cultivated the agrarian Conservatives, called off his war with the Catholics, and outlawed the Social Democrats. To sustain his new policies, he built a new political coalition around protectionism, an alliance between heavy industry and East Elbian agriculture. This linking of aristocratic rye and bourgeois iron gave him a new foundation for domestic power, a base that he used to support his authoritarian regime through another decade.

Bismarck seemed deliberately to encourage fragmentation and irresponsible militancy among economic and political groupings, presumably because it left to him, rather than the parties in Parliament, the role of aggregating particular interests into a national policy. In effect, an authoritarian civilian government, whose popular base and historic mandate were both insecure, maintained itself as the manipulating balancer over and above the economic, social, and political forces of a rapidly evolving society. Bismarck is said to have learned much in these matters from Louis Napoleon. Like France's Second Empire, Bismarck's upstart Reich continually sought to reaffirm its legitimacy, not only through nationalist successes but also through sustaining "modernization" and its benefits. The depression threatened to blight Imperial Germany's new prosperity; hence the vital importance of Bismarck's protectionism.

Control over trade was, in effect, the only practical way to manipulate demand. Neither fiscal nor monetary policy was easily available, for the government's constitutional taxing power was strictly limited, as was its monetary initiative under the prevailing gold standard. In such circumstances, protecting the home market while promoting foreign trade through blocs and dumping was the most promising way to ensure the desperately needed countercyclical markets. The nature of German industry in this period made foreign trade even more significant than later. In a later industrial age of automobiles and other consumer goods, income redistribution could stimulate new demand at home. But Bismarckian Germany was in the age of iron, steel, and machine tools, products without a domestic mass market. New demand – at least that marginal demand essential to profits – was more likely to come from countries still building their railroads and factories – in short, from foreign trade.

Protectionism and Foreign Policy

The new protectionism, in Germany and elsewhere, was not easily compatible with Bismarck's old foreign policy. Tariffs burdened interstate diplomacy with highly competitive trade relations. Increased international friction was nearly inevitable – Russia's bitterness over Germany's agricultural protectionism provides perhaps the most obvious example. More generally, the depression and the wide-spread mercantilist response made a German foreign policy based on the assumption of territorial satiety increasingly incongruous. While in the liberal and prosperous world of 1870, surging German industry could look to open and growing foreign markets, by the midseventies, with all states depressed and seeking relief, foreign markets began closing. Trade thus became increasingly political, and the impulse grew stronger to bring the necessary markets and raw materials into the ambit of political control. Hence, policy gravitated toward self-sufficiency and imperialism. Darwin not Cobden became the prophet for the world's economic order. For Germany, self-sufficiency meant protecting agriculture and industry at home while securing markets and raw materials in Europe or beyond. Thus, the new economic logic led both toward the continental policy of *Mitteleuropa* and the imperialist *Weltpolitik* of William II. Neither was easily compatible with the logic of Bismarck's alliance system, based as it was upon the presumption of a conservative, territorially sated Reich.

As he moved to his protectionist coalition at home, Bismarck himself took a major and probably decisive step toward a new foreign policy. In 1879, over the impassioned opposition of Kaiser William I, Germany made a bilateral alliance with Austria-Hungary, an alliance so firm as to be included in the constitutions of both empires. Why Bismarck should gave taken such a step has continued to puzzle historians. A. J. P. Taylor observes that Bismarck, once having made the alliance, spent the rest of his career trying to avoid its consequences. A close bilateral alliance with Austria clearly ran counter to Bismarck's earlier strategy. It pointed to a German hegemonic bloc in Central Europe; it implied that Big German continental policy Bismarck had so firmly rejected earlier. Conflict with Russia's Balkan ambitions was predictable, as was Russia's turning toward France. To be sure, Bismarck tried to mitigate the consequences with a secret Russian–German Reinsurance

Treaty behind Austria's back. But it could only be a short-term expedient, a temporary preserving of options. The nascent Greater Germany implied in the Austrian alliance would also predictably arouse traditional British instincts against continental hegemony, particularly as a more dynamic German industry was gradually pressing the British in their home and world markets. In short, the Austrian alliance led toward that anti-German diplomatic coalition that Bismarck so wisely feared.

Many considerations seemed to have moved Bismarck, not least, concern over the consequences either of Austria's wandering into the French camp or collapsing and leaving Germany alone to settle with Russia in the Balkans. But economic considerations were interwoven with political ones. Plans for customs unions were much on Bismarck's mind as he tried to think through the international implications of his revolutionary shift in domestic policy. To be sure, the economic arguments cut both ways. Russia offered an even bigger market, but not one that would be so susceptible in the long run to German political control. And in a mercantilist world – the late as opposed to the early 1870s – secure space gained priority over the putative advantages of open trade. In this perspective, the Austrian alliance seems not so much a "mistake" in Bismarck's diplomacy as a move inherent in his mercantilist protectionism. The Austrian alliance was, in effect, a political cartel, the analogue to those industrial cartels with which the Germans, and others, responded to the Great Depression.

German Diplomacy after Bismarck

Analyzing Bismarck's policies suggests two broad options for the empire's political-economic strategy. The first was an economically liberal, territorially satisfied Germany, submitting to comparative advantage in agriculture as well as industry, and counting on free trade both to supply its factories and to sell their products. The second option was a mercantilist and imperialist Germany, seeking self-sufficiency and hence needing hegemony over a space commensurate with its growing production and population. Bismarck began with the first but felt constrained to move toward the second. Bismarck's successor as chancellor, General von Caprivi (1890-95), did his best to return to free trade. Intelligent, reasonable, upright, and decent, Caprivi was highly sensitive to the disruptions and conflicts inherent in economic modernization. Unlike Bismarck, he inclined toward liberal adaptation rather than conservative repression. He was skeptical of Bismarck's fancier diplomatic constructions, like the secret Russian Reinsurance Treaty. But he was no less concerned by Germany's precarious position as a parvenu Great Power in the center of Europe. As a soldier, he was particularly disturbed by the continued flood of emigration out of the Reich. At the same time, he was unimpressed with protectionism as a domestic economic remedy. By 1890, in fact, Germany industry had not pulled out of its slump. Caprivi was particularly alarmed by protectionism's international consequences. If protectionism were not reversed, Caprivi feared, economic warfare would poison Europe's political relations and threaten upstart Germany with the revenge of her neighbors. Hence, to reduce economic conflict, revive German industrial expansion, and provide jobs to keep emigrants at home, Caprivi promoted a liberal European trading bloc. Among his arguments, it should be noted, was concern that a Europe of narrow national economies would some day be dominated by the United States.

Caprivi's "New Course" appealed to a new mix of domestic political forces and perspectives. For a time, he succeeded in mobilizing free-trade interests enough to overcome agrarian opposition and pass a series of relatively liberal trade treaties – principally with Austria-Hungary, Russia, and Britain. At the same time, Caprivi tried to open up and liberalize German society generally. While he was chancellor, the legal repression of the Social Democrats was ended and the government sought to improve the status of Poles and other minorities. The New Course outraged the agrarian conservatives from the start, and soon frightened the haut-bourgeois National Liberals as well. Within five years, Bismarck's coalition of agrarians and heavy industrialists had united to bring down his successor. They were joined by those imperialist, navalist, and Pan-German pressure groups that heavy industry had so assiduously encouraged. Ironically, the long depression finally ended around 1896, to be succeeded by a period of heady trade expansion, during which Caprivi's treaties, which ran until 1902, proved highly beneficial to German industry. Nevertheless, protectionist forces had gained the upper hand, particularly while Bülow was chancellor (1900-9). Hence, when the Caprivi agreements ran out in the early 1900s, Bülow imposed new protectionist treaties upon Russia and the Habsburg Monarchy. Their markets were kept open to German industry while German agriculture was protected. In a few years, these treaties became a major source of diplomatic friction. In Russia and even Austria-Hungary, both old agriculture and developing industry grew increasingly dissatisfied with a status quo so obviously loaded in Germany's favor.

Bülow's policies demonstrate how protectionism had gathered a momentum of its own. The mercantilistic restructuring of industry and politics survived the conditions that had provoked it. Thus, the world economic recovery and boom, which ran from 1896 to 1913, helped promote German imperialism as much as the depression that preceded it. The general mood of exuberant expansion encouraged a proliferation of Germany's worldwide trading interests without changing the mercantilist structures and attitudes fostered by the depression. The optimistic liberal faith in the market never returned. For depression might come back, and only those with a secure territorial base would survive. German economic expansion into the world was thus seen as linked to a concomitant growth of German colonial possessions and naval power. Hence, the *Weltpolitik* particularly associated with Bülow.

In the beginning, Bülow's imperialism was in good part theatrical – belligerent posturing abroad to divert middle- and working-class attention from constitutional reform at home. But what began as a diversion gradually grew into a national obsession. Imperialism was carefully cultivated by groups, in particular the Navy League. Thanks to the league, which was financed by Krupp and inspired by Admiral von Tirpitz, the fleet and its world mission became a great middle-class cause, in distinction from the still aristocratic and European-centered army. A powerful fleet was supposed to make sure that Germany's trade was not pushed out of the nominally independent regions of Latin America or the Near and Far East.

In general, imperialism grew with the democratization of politics. The stunning rise of the Social Democrats, with their organized mass base, pushed the other parties to find a popular base of their own. Imperialism proved a powerful force for mobilizing middle and lower-middle-class voters. Thus, as the Conservative parties used the agrarians and anti-Semites for support, and the Center relied on the various Catholic associations, the National Liberals turned to imperialism. By the second decade of the twentieth century bourgeois opinion was thoroughly impregnated with the notion that for future growth Germany required a major territorial sphere of its own in the world, a sphere comparable to those of Britain, Russia, and the United States.

In summary, with so aggressive a foreign policy springing, it seems, from the inner compulsions of Germany's political and economic system, any return to a "satisfied" liberal foreign policy was improbable. The conservative protectionism that Bismarck had fostered in response to compelling economic changes made his liberal foreign policy obsolescent even before 1890. He himself was the first to change it. Caprivi could not turn back and Germany was on the path to war.

Bismarck's Diplomacy: Long-Run Consequences

Bismarck, it seems, had no magic formula. Indeed, after 1871, his diplomatic genius perhaps did his country more harm than good. His own solution was an unstable interlude, incompatible with Germany's dynamism within a shrinking world. Bismarck's parvenu great power would either make room for itself or be crushed. Bismarck, of course, did quite enough for one lifetime. It was enough to create the Second Reich without at the same time solving all its inherent problems. But by the end of his rule, it might be argued, Bismarck had already seriously weakened Germany for the struggle that his Reich had made inevitable. A number of hopeful options were already gone.

Annexing Alsace-Lorraine, for example, had made France a permanent enemy, too big for Bismarck's Germany to crush permanently. An unbroken France, carrying the grievance of lost territories, could be expected to await its revenge. Menawhile, one of the major possibilities for Germany's future, a European bloc based in Franco-German understanding, was foreclosed.

Secondly, it was Bismarck, after all, who cemented the fateful alliance with Austria-Hungary. Russia was bound to react, and France, in due course, to find an ally. The German army would then face a war on two fronts.

If political-economic compulsions meant that France and Russia were both to be enemies, every effort ought to, have been made to ally with Britain. But Bismarck, although he often joined diplomatic forces with Disraeli

and Salisbury, never established genuinely friendly relations with the British — no more than his hapless successor, Bülow, who finally pushed Britain into the arms of its
old enemies, Russia and France, or Bethmann-Hollweg,
who reaped the whirlwind. But at least Bismarck's successors, driven by imperialist ambitions beyond Europe, had
better reasons for quarreling with Britain. Bismarck not
only held the British at arm's length, but cynically cultivated that popular hatred of Britain that proved a major
constraint for German diplomacy. Conflict with Britain
was, of course, inherent in the industrial tariffs that were
the bourgeois counterpart to protection for agriculture.
Hence, it is said, Germany's double conflict with Russia
and Britain was inherent in the protectionist coalition by
which Bismarck sustained his authoritarian regime.

Something of the persisting Anglo-German coolness
can also be laid to the style that Bismarck fostered in Germany's diplomacy and indeed in its domestic politics as
well. German statecraft seems to have taken a certain perverse pleasure in affecting a diplomatic style that combined
deceit with shock. Along with this Nietzschean enthusiasm
for brutal craftiness went a lack of restraint in language, a
taste for hyperbole that William II developed to an almost
hysterical degree. But Bismarck himself had many of the
same traits. From the first, the Bismarckian style carried
an undertone of hysteria, suggesting perhaps the great
strains that Prussia's rapid rise placed upon Germany's
society, culture, and political institutions.

To be sure, underlying hysteria was common enough
everywhere at the end of the last century. From the late
seventies, British politics began to exhibit an extraordinarily virulent factiousness, only temporarily soothed by Salisbury. The same virulent contentiousness came to character-
ize France and Russia. But only Bismarck seems to have
elevated abandoned factiousness to the organizing constitutional principle of national politics. With habits of com-

promise and arts of conciliation so little cultivated, order and measure could be brought to public policy only through an authoritarian mediator. It would be foolish to lay these characteristics of German politics to Bismarck alone, for they obviously had broad causes. Perhaps the dynamic and unformed state of German politics and society would not have permitted anything other than his brand of authoritarian leadership to succeed. Nevertheless, by developing this style of government into a great art, and endowing it with his own success and prestige, Bismarck helped confirm his countrymen in their worst habits and handicapped their capacity to adapt to domestic and international change. Bismarck, of course, had an aggressive style but a conservative foreign policy. His successors were often aggressive in policy as well as tone, not a winsome combination. But this aggressive policy, as I have been suggesting, seems implicit in the general direction of German and world economic development, an evolution apparent in Bismarck's own time. An economically expansive Germany was not going to remain locked up in its Central European box.

Under these circumstances, the significance of style can easily be exaggerated. It is sometimes said that subtle cultural misunderstandings continually antagonized relations between British and German elites. More likely, they understood each other all too well. All great powers in the late nineteenth century were increasingly mercantilist and imperialist. Their domestic and foreign policies were not merely reactions to German initiatives. Even if all Germans had been well-mannered liberal constitutionalists, the other Great Powers would have been unlikely to make room gracefully for a politically united and economically dynamic Germany. In a world system of rival imperialisms, a world – after all – that Germany had not created, Bismarck's Reich was almost certain to become "aggressive" against a status quo still reflecting the earlier predominance of others. Thoughtful Germans knew this. For Max Weber in 1895, German unification would be only ". . . a youthful prank indulged in by the nation in its old age . . . better left undone if it was meant to be the end and not the starting point of a German *Weltmachtpolitik*."[1] By 1916, he had not blinked at the consequences: "If we had not wished to risk this war we could have left the Reich unfounded and continued as a nation of small states."[2]

From this perspective, Bismarck's conservative foreign policy was not an alternative that his less skillful successors abandoned. At best, it only delayed the catastrophe that his creation of a new German Reich was fated to bring down upon Europe. Indeed, Bismarck himself took the fatal steps that were to link France and Russia in a union to destroy Germany. Perhaps he was at least more realistic than his successors, who kept hoping Britain might save them. Whether a bolder policy after 1870 might have succeeded remains a fascinating if obviously impossible question. Perhaps, as Hitler was to argue, Imperial Germany should have absorbed Austria and pressed earlier for a showdown with Russia. A great territorial sphere in the East might have given mercantilist Germany the space and leisure it craved. By 1914, it was too late. Germany's commercial expansion meant that France and Russia were joined by Britain. In the end, Imperial Germany was too aggressive to be accepted peacefully and perhaps not aggressive enough to win security by the sword.

1 Max Weber, *Gesammelte Politische Schriften* (Munich: Drei Masten Verlag, 1921), p 29.
2 Ibid., p. 92.

3

Germany and the First World War

Introduction: The Problem of Continuity

Historians, almost by definition, search for continuity. In modern German history, the problems of continuity are perhaps more intriguing and troubling than for any other country. What, for example, happened to the old Germany of "thinkers and poets" after Bismarck's Germany of "blood and iron"? What was the link between Bismarck and the First World War? What was the continuity of foreign policy from Imperial to Weimar to Nazi Germany, from Bethmann-Hollweg to Stresemann to Hitler? Or, nowadays, what has happened to the Nazi past in the present societies of East or West Germany?

To come to our own particular preoccupation: How much continuity was there in German "aggressiveness"? Before Bismarck, no one could single out the modern Germans as uniquely aggressive, particularly by comparison with the British, French, or Russians. Bismarck himself, for all his saber rattling, carefully restricted his ambitions to a conservative version of a German national state. Even his most notable lapse, Alsace-Lorraine, figured as a traditional part of Germany acquired by France during the many wars of the seventeenth and eighteenth centuries. And Bismarck did not, incidentally, start the war with France. After Bismarck came that liberal and peaceful general, Caprivi. Nevertheless, by the early twentieth century, the Germans were already thought uncommonly aggressive. Why? Bülow's theatrical *Weltpolitik* did, of course, lead to some minor but abrasive colonial undertakings and confrontations. Even his relatively prudent successor, Bethmann-Hollweg, had his own Moroccan crisis in 1911. A good deal of Germany's reputation for aggressiveness must probably be laid to the prevalent German style – a traditional Prussian military stiffness caricatured by middle-class imitators. And there was Kaiser William II, exhorting his troops to behave like "Huns." Still, Imperial Germany's colonial efforts remained, after all, minor in comparison with those of Britain, France, or even the United States. And off the public platform, William's predilections were far more cautious than his language. Before 1914, in short, German aggressiveness seems at most potential rather than actual.

The year 1914 was the watershed. The worst suspicions about the German character seemed amply fulfilled. Those remaining doubts that helped nourish appeasement were ultimately squelched by Hitler. Since the Second World War, much of German historical scholarship has continually emphasized the similarities between Imperial and Nazi "war aims," and thereby linked Imperial ambitions with Nazi crimes. Thus a continuity of war guilt seems to tie Bethmann-Hollweg to Hitler. The link is certainly convenient, particularly when forged by the Germans themselves. But how much continuity was there, in fact, in this German aggression? How "responsible" was Germany for the First World War?

The question of "war guilt" began to preoccupy historians almost from the moment the fighting started in 1914.

A vast body of research and argumentation presents a wide range of hypotheses. Understandably, the subject has often been bitterly controversial and highly partisan, an ideological issue among countries and also within them. So sweeping and complex an event lends itself to many forms of analysis. The conflict had broad origins not only in a long-range political and economic power struggle among the major states, but also in the whole process of economic, political, and social "modernization" in all Western societies. But such general explanations, however revealing, are never sufficient. Important tensions are seldom absent among closely related states, and few modern societies are ever free from serious internal strains. The springs of international conflict are always wound. What releases them to hurl states into bloody battle? For the answer, we must still turn to the diplomatic and "Cabinet" historians. After over a half century of study, what can they tell us?

The best cosmopolitan surveys, of which Luigi Albertini's *Origins of the War of 1914* remains a superb example, make clear that all the major powers shared a heavy responsibility in 1914. If Austria-Hungary and Germany precipitated the confrontation, France and Russia showed little inclination to avoid it. And if, in truth, Britain wished to stop the war, its diplomacy was culpably incompetent. Before turning in detail to Germany's role, it may be useful to touch on the motives of the other major powers.

Europe's Great Powers in the July Crisis

For Austria-Hungary, the war seemed justified by the need to deal decisively with Serbia. From Vienna, Serbia was seen as the Balkan Piedmont. Serbian agitation, encouraged by Russia, had been undermining the loyalty of the empire's Slavic subjects. Serbia's victories in the 1912 and 1913 Balkan wars were seriously damaging the Dual Monarchy's prestige, an all-important asset for a dynastic

empire without a national base. Powerful elements in the
Habsburg government – in particular the imperial chief-
of-staff, Conrad von Hötzendorff – demanded drastic military and political action to reverse the empire's deterioration. Many who shared these views, including the assassi-
nated heir to the throne, Franz Ferdinand, had been pressing for a "trialist" solution to the Dual Monarchy's constitutional problems. Once Serbia was crushed, a domestically
autonomous South Slavic kingdom was to enjoy equal
status with Austrian and Hungarian realms. For years, however, the Hungarians had impeded decisive military or constitutional action. The Hungarians, it should be noted, generally had outside support from the Prussians. This Prussian–Hungarian special relationship was, in effect, a principal means by which Germany kept Austria in line. But economic tension between Vienna and Berlin was growing in
the Balkans, particularly as German commercial interests
tended to flirt with the Serbians at the same time as
German diplomatic policy discouraged Austrian retribu-
tion. By the summer of 1914 the Germans, for reasons
developed below, no longer felt inclined to inhibit Austrian
wrath against Serbia. On the contrary, unless Austria acted
against Serbia, the Germans argued, the Dual Monarchy
could no longer be taken seriously as a Great Power, and
Germany might look elsewhere for allies. The Austrian
activist party, backed for once by the Germans, finally prevailed. The Dual Monarchy, its internal inhibitions overcome with German help, then became immovable, even
against Bethmann's last-minute reversal.

If the Central Powers precipitated the crisis, the Allies
cannot be said to have done much to avoid it. The Russians
shared a large part of the immediate responsibility. The
minister in Serbia, Hartwig, had for years played a highly
inflammatory role. The Russian government had not
exactly approved, but had not stopped him, even though
Habsburg vulnerability made war predictable. Russian

public opinion, and even the czar's own court, were rife with Pan-Slavic enthusiasm, which the government was not strong enough to resist. The foreign minister, Sazonov, was weak, excitable, and consumed by a great hatred for the Austrians. When the July crisis came, he lost control to the military, whose standing plans made mobilization against Austria impossible without simultaneous mobilization against Germany. Thus the fatal sequence that ended with the Battle of the Marne. Quite apart from the Balkan imbroglio, Russo-German relations had steadily deteriorated for economic reasons. Russian grain growers resented German protectionism. And as Russia began to industrialize on a grand scale, traditional German economic penetration seemed less and less tolerable. Finally, Germany's increasing penetration of the Turkish Empire threatened Russia's long-range ambitions there and hence aroused more and more venomous resentment.

The French, although not directly involved with Serbia, nevertheless played a provocative rule. Paléologue, France's Ambassador in Saint Petersburg, probably misled the Quai d'Orsay and certainly encouraged Russian belligerence. Poincaré, the president, and Viviani, the premier visited the czar just before the Austrian ultimatum. Indeed, the ultimatum was held up until they had left. Interestingly, records of these talks seem to have disappeared. The crisis broke while Poincaré and Viviani were slowly and circuitously returning to France. Viviani, finally back in Paris, found a tremendous popular outpouring demanding war. His conciliatory initiatives were swept aside. The critical question was what Britain would do. Paul Cambon, ambassador in London, had carefully cultivated Britain's moral obligation not to desert France in a war with Germany. Gray's indolent reaction permitted France to take the initiative in supporting Russia and thus, in effect, Britain allowed itself to be led into war.

From a longer-range perspective, France's role could not

help but be conditioned by the determination to regain Alsace-Lorraine. Poincaré, for example, was a Lorrainer. And even for many Frenchmen disinclined to wage war for the lost provinces, some showdown seemed inevitable. A rapidly growing Germany was a mortal threat to a stagnant France. Either Germany would be defeated or France reduced to a vassal. France had patiently knit together a grand alliance; the moment had come to use it.

The more the diplomatic historian unwinds the motives, perceptions, and interests of the major actors, and lays bare the many intractable conflicts gathering for so long a time, the more a general war seems to have been almost inevitable. Russia's pursuit of Pan-Slavic ambitions in the Balkans threatened the very survival of the troubled Austro-Hungarian Empire. How could the Balkan situation have been resolved? Bismarck sometimes seemed to encourage Austria and Russia to partition the peninsula between them. Russia, he thought, might be supported in its old ambition to control the straits; the Balkans, or at least the western part of them, could then be left to Austria. Pan-Slavism stood in the way. As the czar's monarchy grew weaker and more obviously incompetent, it was less and less able to resist the Pan-Slavic pressure of public opinion. After 1905, the Russian government was probably too weak to make a definitive settlement. The same may be said of the Habsburg Empire. Stabilizing both the monarchy and the Balkan situation would probably have required some kind of Triple Federation. But the empire could never overcome its own internal paralysis. Comparisons between Austria-Hungary and the Ottoman Empire were becoming less and less farfetched.

In summary, with Russia probably unable to stop fomenting conflict and Austria seemingly unable to take the initiative toward an internally viable resolution, continuing conflict in the Balkans seems to have been unavoidable. With Austria increasingly desperate, and Serbia increasingly bold, Austria's direct intervention was almost inevitable, as was a strong Russian reaction. With the Franco-Russian Entente, rooted in a fundamental antagonism between France and Germany and a growing antagonism between Germany and Russia, an Austro-Russian Balkan war was fated to become general. Could anything have broken the chain?

Britain's Critical Role

July 1914, was not, of course, the first Balkan crisis. Balkan issues had plagued the last quarter of the nineteenth century and local Balkan wars had occurred in 1909, 1912, and 1913. Why did 1914 lead to a general war? Normally, two powers had held back the others — Germany and Britain. In 1914, their bilateral negotiations went on until the last minute. Yet, in the end, they failed to collaborate. Why? The German chancellor, Bethmann-Hollweg, blamed the British, as his emotional farewell to Goschen, the British ambassador, makes vivid:

> It was a crime that Russia forced war upon us while we were still negotiating between Vienna and Petersburg, and Russia's and France's war against Germany was enough of a disaster. But this war turned into an unlimited world catastrophe only through England's participation. . . . It was in London's hand to curb French revanchism and Pan-Slav chauvinism. It has not done so, but has, rather, repeatedly egged them on. And now England has actively helped them. Germany, the Emperor, and the government were peace-loving; that, the Ambassador knew as well as I. We entered the war with a clear conscience, but England's responsibility was monumental.[1]

Bethmann-Hollweg's bitter disappointment was understandable. Britain's entry marked the defeat of his whole diplomatic strategy, not only in the July crisis, but from the beginning of his chancellorship in 1909. Bethmann

[1] Konrad Jarausch, *The Enigmatic Chancellor: Bethmann-Hollweg and the Hubris of Imperial Germany* (New Haven, Conn.: Yale University Press, 1973), pp. 176–7.

had counted upon cultivating a special relationship with Britain both to neutralize the Franco-Russian "encirclement" and to achieve peacefully Germany's long-range imperial aims. Britain's friendship, he believed, would ultimately let Germany have these aims without a war. Bethmann gambled that Britain would continue to restrain the Entente in 1914. British hesitations fed his hopes to the last moment. Throughout the July crisis, Grey, the foreign secretary, appears to have been remarkably slow-witted and diffident. Only very slowly did he seem to grasp the inexorable logic leading from Austrian intervention against Serbia to Russian intervention against Austria, followed by the entry of Germany and France – a contest, once started, from which Britain could not stand aloof without seeing the European balance of power altered irreparably. A decisive Britain, making clear either its support or nonsupport, might conceivably have prevented the conflict. To be sure, with the desperation prevailing in Vienna, St. Petersburg, and indeed Berlin, even a resolute Britain might not have smothered the crisis. In any event, Grey procrastinated until the chance was gone.

What can explain this British diffidence? Something can always be laid to British incompetence. British statesmanship and diplomacy were uncertain at best. British ambassadors were almost universally bad. But diffidence is frequently complex; its causes often lie somewhere between muddleheadedness and guile. Bethmann's expectations relied upon a certain British goodwill toward the Reich's ambitions and a relative detachment from the Franco-Russian struggle to contain Germany on the Continent. But Germany's commercial aggressiveness and general ambition to be a "world" power had steadily eroded whatever British goodwill and detachment may once have existed. German world aspirations, carried to their logical conclusion, seemed fated to bring the German and British empires either to war or alliance. At the turn of the century and intermittently thereafter, some British leaders, chiefly Joseph Chamberlain, had toyed with conciliating Germany; but neither side ever seemed quite serious. By 1907, as Sir Eyre Crowe's famous Foreign Office memorandum suggests, the British were growing less and less accommodating. According to Crowe, who knew Germany well and indeed had a German wife, German aspirations were infinite. The German Empire, he argued, was the heir of Prussia, whose remarkable rise was "systematic territorial aggrandizement achieved mainly at the point of the sword . . . deliberately embarked upon by ambitious rulers or statesmen. . . ."[2] Once it became a Great Power, Prussia immediately aspired to be a world power. Such a state could not be appeased:

> There is one road which, if past experience is any guide to the future, will most certainly not lead to any permanent improvement of relations with any Power, least of all Germany, and which must therefore be abandoned: that is the road paved with graceful British concessions . . .[3]

The British, of course, might equally well have applied the same logic to the United States, as the Germans hoped they would. And because the United States was so much bigger, alliance with Germany was the natural step to preserve a "world" balance. Such speculations were doubtless too excessive for the British imagination, already attracted to the notion of a British–American Special Relationship, a sort of Anglo-Saxon world imperium that would coopt the American cousins. So Britain spurned Germany to join France and Russia. Crushing Germany, of course, proved ruinously expensive and, as the Germans predicted, left the United States the real victor.

Was Crowe wrong? Could Britain have preserved more of its world position by conciliating Germany? Such a ques-

---

[2] Imanuel Geiss, *German Foreign Policy 1871–1914* (London: Routledge and Kegan Paul, 1976), p. 195.
[3] Ibid., p. 200.

tion opens a heady vista of historical speculation. The two wars that so weakened Europe – Britain and Germany together – might have been avoided. A more equal world balance might have contained the exuberant energies of the nascent superpowers – Russia and the United States. Such a line of argument, however, assumes what Crowe explicitly denied: that Germany's "aggressive" aims might have been appeased and stabilized within some generally acceptable world framework. This brings us back to Germany's responsibility for the First World War, but raises the question to another level: What might it have taken to appease Imperial Germany?

Germany's War Aims: General Preoccupations

In recent years the question of Imperial Germany's "war aims" has once again generated intense scholarly attention and debate. Analysis of these "aims" falls naturally into three distinct parts: first, the goals of the German government during the July Crisis – that moment of decision to back Austria that Kurt Riezler, Bethmann-Hollweg's private secretary and close adviser, described as Bethmann's "leap into the dark" dictated by the "most serious duty";[4] second, the formulation and evolution of the government's aims after the war had begun; and finally the broader geopolitical and economic preoccupations, both of the regime and of the public at large, which made up the context within which German policy was formulated. Much confusion comes from mixing up these three questions.

Perhaps it is best to begin with the general climate. Public opinion was widely preoccupied with broad geopolitical questions about Germany's future. The very nature of Germany's industrial development – in which large-scale organization, long-range planning, and close state–business cooperation had played so great a part – helps to

---

[4] Jarausch, op. cit., p. 159.

explain this preoccupation with grand plans. Moreover, a number of mass pressure groups, like the Pan-German, Army, and Navy leagues, often financed by big business and appealing to bourgeois opinion, existed to promote a public "understanding" of Germany's geopolitical needs. Various large-scale interest groups, like the Agrarian League, the Federation of German Industries, and the Hansa League, also frequently concerned themselves with geopolitical questions. Bourgeois political parties, searching for a popular base to counter the Social Democrats, often closely allied themselves with the various imperialist mass associations. On the whole, these groups were aggressive in their ambitions for Germany's future. They were also fearful. They looked enviously at the vast potential of the British and Russian empires, as well as the United States. Unless Germany could break out of its continental straitjacket, they reasoned, it would inevitably be outclassed and reduced to a satellite.

How influential was geopolitics in actual policy? William II's addiction to geopolitical rhetoric perhaps exaggerates its significance. In practice, "William the Timid," as he came to be called, showed considerable appreciation both of Germany's precarious diplomatic situation and of his own shortcomings as "Supreme Warlord." But whereas government policies were more restrained than the pronouncements either of the kaiser or of the intellectuals who set the tone for the mass pressure groups, the drive to be a "world" power was nevertheless a major element in the general intellectual context within which German foreign policy was formulated.

The various writings of Kurt Riezler give a comprehensive and sober exposition of Germany's geopolitical preoccupations, as well as an idea of the broader perspectives of those responsible for policy. Riezler's general views were commonplace for the period: History saw the rise and fall of peoples. Each sought room and resources to develop its inherent potential. Resources were generally more limited than ambitions and thus international collisions and conflicts were inevitable. If a rising nation could not win enough places for itself, it would decline and stagnate. All these commonplace Darwinist notions were, among other things, part of the heritage bequeathed by the Great Depression.

Riezler's more novel speculations lay in his theory of how the contemporary international system adjusted its conflicts, and, in particular, the function of armaments and diplomatic crises in that adjustment. International relations had become highly static, Riezler noted, thanks to an all-embracing system of alliances and a very high level of armaments. Forces among the Great Powers were so finely balanced that quick and easy victories were unlikely, and risks on all sides high. With the system thus biased against war, adjustments tended to take place through diplomatic confrontations. In these confrontations, Riezler argued, the strong rising power would have better nerves and thus could hope to win at least marginal concessions. Wars were most likely when a declining Great Power, feeling its interests threatened directly, decided on a show of force to reestablish its prestige. In effect, Riezler developed an early theory of brinkmanship. He used the earlier Balkan crises as examples of how diplomatic confrontation and limited proxy wars brought systemic adjustment. Not surprisingly, a number of historians have found these ideas a key to Bethmann-Hollweg's diplomacy in July 1914.

Before moving to the July Crisis, two other major elements in the government's general perspectives need discussion. The first was Germany's economic situation, which was thought to be deteriorating; the second the military situation, which was thought to be growing desperate.

As we know, from 1870 to 1913, Germany's industry grew at a breathtaking pace. The British, while still ahead in some respects, were clearly losing ground. France, if a major financial power, was limited in its industrial growth to a more measured pace. Russia was beginning to grow very rapidly, but was still well behind. In many spheres, the Germans were rivaled only by the Americans, already by 1883 the world's largest economy. But Germany, without the huge and protected American domestic market, was far more of a force in the world economy and far more dependent upon it. Overall, Germany's foreign trade increased at a rate unmatched by any other country. Although the balance of its huge trade was unfavorable, Germany's growing earnings as a provider of commercial services, especially merchant shipping, more than covered the deficit.

By 1914, however, Germany seemed to be approaching a crisis in its commercial relations. Despite a marked shift to overseas markets, Germany's foreign trade in 1914 was still three-quarters within Europe. Bülow's favorable trade agreements with Russia and Austria had safeguarded important European markets for Germany's industries, while still permitting protection for its agriculture. By 1914, the agreements were soon to expire and their renewal was uncertain. Over the years, industrial and agricultural interests in both Russia and Austria-Hungary had grown increasingly restive. Russian industry, nourished by a massive flow of French capital, was promoting its own protectionist design and expecting to push the Germans out of their traditional eastern markets, of vital importance to the great Silesian steel complex. At the same time, the Ruhr steel industry apparently feared it might become dependent upon French ore. Attempts to guarantee that supply were meeting ominous political resistance. Various German economic designs in Turkey, moreover, were suddenly foundering in competition with more abundant French capital. In general, the exuberant sense of growth and power that had accompanied the astonishing development of the German economy in the postdepression boom years was giving way, by 1914, to a gloomy view of shrinking possibilities and hostile encirclement. Many signs seemed to indicate a general world economic downturn in the offing.

The Germans looked to political solutions. A more active *Weltpolitik*, they believed, could open overseas markets and gain colonies for markets and raw materials. And German leadership in Europe could promote a continental bloc to prevent discrimination against German goods in neighboring markets. Not surprisingly, once war had begun, plans for a European trade bloc in *Mitteleuropa* and for German colonies in *Mittelafrika* loomed large in the popular lists of war aims.

However uneasy the government may have felt about trade, its most pressing concern was with Germany's military position. Since the Franco-Russian political and military agreements of 1893 and 1894, the German General Staff had had to calculate for a war on two fronts. Their solution, the famous Schlieffen Plan of 1905, called for a lightning strike into France through Belgium, while Austria-Hungary and minimal German forces held the Russians in the east. France was to be defeated quickly, before Russia could fully mobilize. After 1909, and especially after 1913, the assumptions of this strategy began to crumble. The growing power of Serbia was expected to drain an increasing proportion of Austro-Hungarian forces away from the Russian front, while the increasing fragility of the Triple Alliance with Italy might well divert many more. The French, moreover, sharply increased their military manpower in 1913 by extending conscription from two to three years. Above all, the German calculations were being upset by Russia's rearmament, designed to be completed by 1917. The czarist regime, financed by the French, was not only greatly increasing its military expenditures, and thus presumably improving the effectiveness of its military forces, but also building a railway network to permit their rapid concentration on the Western border. As a result, the calculations of the Schlieffen Plan were growing obsolete. By 1912, the General Staff began to advocate "preventive" war.

Bethmann, however, was sensitive both to the terrible risks of war and to the remaining possibilities of diplomacy. Improving diplomatic relations with the British, he argued, counterbalanced the deteriorating military position vis-à-vis France and Russia. A growing Anglo-German understanding, he maintained, would distance Britain from the Entente, satisfy Germany's legitimate colonial interests, and thus make so desperately hazardous a war unnecessary. But the secret Anglo-Russian naval talks of June 1914, discovered by German espionage, shook Bethmann's position badly. Thus, at the moment of the Sarajevo crisis in July 1914, the chancellor was under great pressure to act. Probably more than anything else, this military pressure explains his fateful decision to push Austria-Hungary into war with Serbia.

The Government's Aims in the July Crisis: Bethmann-Hollweg's Gamble

Bethmann's brinkmanship at Sarajevo was a double gamble. If the first part succeeded, the Russians would back down as they had before – either because they were still unready for war or because the French, and especially the British, might not support them. In that case, Serbia would be crushed. Germany's only major ally, Austria-Hungary, would have a new lease on life, while mutual recriminations would gravely undermine the encircling Entente. If the initial gamble failed, the German army would have the war with France and Russia for which it clamored, and Germany would gamble on a quick military victory. Diplomatic and domestic circumstances would be at their most favorable. Austria-Hungary's support would be assured, for the Dual Monarchy could hardly opt out of a war it had started. Domestic unity would be assured as well. To the German public, Russia, not Germany, would seem the aggressor. The whole country, the Socialist working class included, could be united in a war against Slav "imperialism."

Bethmann lost the initial gamble the moment war began. The Entente did hold together and did go to war. Hence, no doubt, Bethmann's bitterness with Goschen. Bethmann had overestimated his own influence with the British, and underestimated how far they were already committed.

Bethmann also lost his second gamble. There was no quick, decisive military victory. The French won the Battle of the Marne. They fought brilliantly and the Germans made mistakes, but Britain's military contribution also proved larger and more determined than anticipated. The British had more unpleasant surprises for Bethmann. Contrary to the usual proprieties, private German overseas property was confiscated; industrial patents appropriated; trade interests destroyed; and an unprecedented civilian blockade imposed. The British, in effect, settled in for a long all-out world war – an excellent opportunity, after all, to crush Germany's hitherto rapidly progressing international economic challenge. The hapless Germans, their overseas trade destroyed, belatedly recognized Britain's great advantages in sustaining a long war.

German Aims after War Began: Bethmann-Hollweg versus the Annexationists

Whereas the Bethmann government's immediate goals in the July Crisis seem relatively clear, the evolution of aims during the fighting is far more obscure. At home, Bethmann's power was deteriorating and he was increasingly forced to maneuver among clamoring groups.

Abroad, his stated positions were meant to be starting points for negotiations. Thus it is difficult to know what the chancellor really wanted or whether his aims would have prevailed in a German victory. In any event, Bethmann's various formulations of "war aims" have to be seen in the light of Germany's evolving military, diplomatic, and domestic political situation. Initially, Bethmann wanted victory without war. Once war had started, he hoped for a quick and favorable military decision, followed by negotiations with the British. As a quick military victory eluded the Germans, Bethmann hoped for a negotiated settlement that might salvage enough long-range ambitions to appease the German public and justify its terrible sacrifices. But as he was gradually to discover, Germany was no longer able to negotiate even a return to the status quo ante.

Bethmann-Hollweg's early statement of war aims — the famous September Program of 1914 — came after the diplomatic gamble had failed and Britain's earnest involvement was clear, but before the hope of a quick military victory was dashed. The September Program was actually an internal document to coordinate government policies, and, in particular, to contain the more extreme ambitions of the military. Bethmann's task was to concoct a formula that might translate a quick military victory into a stable settlement. The settlement had to leave Germany strong enough to deter the British from a long war of attrition. But the settlement could not be so severe that British resistance would grow desperate. .

Not surprisingly, the formula tried to respond to the prevailing geopolitical preoccupations with Germany's military and economic "encirclement." Bethmann's announced aim was to make continental Germany secure for all time. France was to be defeated decisively and rendered unable to launch a war of revenge. Specifically, heavy and protracted reparations were to be imposed, and some frontier territory of military significance was to be taken as well as the rich iron mines of Longwy-Briey. Belgium was to become a German vassal state. Holland was to be brought into a "closer relationship" with the Reich without, however, any "feeling of compulsion." An integrated continental economic system including Germany, Austria-Hungary, the Low Countries, "Poland," and perhaps also France, Italy, and Scandinavia was to realize *Mitteleuropa*. Russia was to be pushed as far as possible away from the German frontier and its hold over the non-Russian vassal peoples broken. A continuous central African colonial empire was to realize *Mittelafrika*. These political-economic ideas reflected not only the general geopolitical preoccupations discussed above, but the particular influence of Walther Rathenau, the industrialist and banker. Significantly, Rathenau was one of the first to point out how ruinous the war would be for Germany's world commercial position. Hence, presumably, his interest in securing a large common market for Germany in Europe. Nevertheless, even in anticipating a military victory, Germany's actual territorial expansion in Europe was to be relatively modest.

Although the September Program obviously reflected long-standing geopolitical preoccupations, as well as momentary tactical concerns, French military successes soon made it irrelevant. No doubt the September Program reflected something of what the Germans might actually have demanded had they won an early and decisive victory. Even then, of course, many other considerations would have intervened, in particular, the strong desire to avoid a long war with Britain and Russia. In any event, as Bethmann quickly grew skeptical of the chances for a decisive German victory, he began looking toward some sort of negotiated settlement with at least some if not all of the Entente. His negotiating prospects were severely constrained, however, by the mounting demands among the military for extensive German annexations of neighboring territories. Thanks to lavish financing by important elements of big business, these demands were widely propagated and well rooted in middle-class opinion generally. The resultant fever was amply reflected in the Reichstag. Bethmann with difficulty frustrated demands for precise formulation of war aims, but dared not be too unforthcoming lest he be swept aside and the initiative pass completely to the military extremists.

Bethmann's differences with the annexationists lay more in means than ends. He too wanted Germany to be a world power. He was no less determined to break the Franco-Russian "encirclement" and replace it with some form of German hegemony on the Continent. But, like Riezler and Rathenau, he had a more measured and sophisticated view of how German political and economic hegemony could be structured and exercised. Like the more enlightened business figures, Bethmann appreciated the possibilities of that liberal, indirect imperialism so perfected by the British and Americans in many parts of the world. By contrast, the German army, usually seconded by heavy industry, sought to annex directly as much territory as possible.

Bethmann's relative moderation sprang not only from a more sophisticated view of how victory could be exploited, but also from a more realistic notion of Germany's actual military, diplomatic, and domestic situation. To start with the domestic situation: Various military and other Rightist elements thought the war was a heaven-sent opportunity to extirpate the Social Democratic party and perhaps the parliamentary system altogether. Bethmann, by contrast, saw the integration of the Social Democrats and workers generally as his vital political task. Hence his eagerness to stress the war's "defensive" nature. Workers would fight for Germany's right to live, but not for annexationist ambitions deep in France and Russia. More and more, Bethmann found himself caught between his concern for holding working-class support and the middle-class annexationist fever. His scheme for an indirect economic empire, "*Mittel-europa*," its feasibility attacked within the government for all sorts of technical reasons, was characteristic of Bethmann's search for formulas to contain the annexationists without alienating the workers – one of his celebrated "diagonals" between powerful forces pressing in opposite directions.

As the war continued, Bethmann's own sympathies brought him closer and closer to the Social Democrats, who were themselves edging toward the center. Bethmann was profoundly moved by the spirit of patriotic loyalty and sacrifice among the working classes and increasingly disgusted by the undisciplined posturing of the German military, industrial, and professional elites. After a long struggle, he secured in 1917 the kaiser's commitment to reform the undemocratic election system of the Prussian *Landtag*, still the privileged bastion of German reaction. Had the reform occurred, it would have broken the back of the reactionary agrarians and removed a long-standing obstacle to a more responsive parliamentary constitution. Ironically, Bethmann's triumphant announcement to the Reichstag came on the day before the Russian Revolution.

In Bethmann's view, Germany's military situation provided another powerful incentive for moderate policies. He rapidly grew disillusioned with the military's apparently infinite capacity for self-deception, the source of that fatuous optimism that fed the annexationist fever. Yet, as the terrible sacrifices mounted both at the front and at home, Bethmann dared not reveal his own gloomy assessment for fear of destroying civilian morale and perhaps provoking a revolution. Meanwhile, he tried to use censorship to suppress the annexationist propaganda.

Moderation also best served Germany's diplomatic situation, Bethmann believed. The territorial ambitions of the military and their annexationist allies were not only hopelessly unrealistic, but would hamstring German diplomacy in extricating the country from the coming disaster. Germany might still trade its early gains for a tolerable European settlement.

Had Bethmann's only problem been the annexationists, he would have had an easier task. His principal difficulty, however, lay with the Allies, the British in particular. Because they controlled the seas and were better suited for a lengthy war of attrition than the Germans, their eventual victory seemed likely. After so many sacrifices, they wanted the Reich decisively defeated, rather than left in its prewar position of potential continental hegemony. But the Germans, whatever their long-range prospects, were far from beaten in the field until the very end. They could always hope for one great victory that would shatter Allied morale. Under the circumstances, negotiations were unlikely to succeed.

Thus, Bethmann, if he had a realistic view of Germany's predicament, had few prospects for extricating the country from it. Because he could never demonstrate how moderation in war aims and conduct would yield positive results, he was always on the defensive, always forced to give way to the military's desperate gambles. Thus, for example, he managed to delay the submarine campaign in order not to spoil the American peace initiatives. But the Britsh, confident of victory, had no real interest in negotiations. Finally, Tirpitz had his way. Bethmann, of course, was right about the submarine campaign. Submarines did not win the war and America's entry confirmed Germany's defeat. But against Tirpitz's optimism, however ill-founded or dishonest, Bethmann himself had nothing to offer. Similarly, Bethmann stood for moderation when the czarist regime collapsed. A moderate settlement, he argued, would release desperately needed troops and show German goodwill. It might prepare the way for a negotiated western settlement. It would be the last chance before the Americans arrived. However reasonable the arguments otherwise, their presumption of successful negotiations with the Western Allies had become implausible.

In retrospect, Bethmann's position seems hopeless. After the failure of his 1914 gamble, he had no diplomatic strategy with serious prospects for success. Once the fighting got underway, there was no alternative to total war. At the end as at the start, Bethmann was still vainly hoping for the Allies to save him. But they were not interested in negotiating anything but a surrender. Hence Bethmann's strategy, if more realistic than the military's, was no less bankrupt. His celebrated policy of "diagonals" was essentially a compromise between hopeless alternatives. In the end, he alienated everyone. His moderation exasperated the military, whereas the compromises necessary to remain in office finally undercut his credibility with moderates and progressives. Ultimately, the Reichstag deserted him, even the Social Democrats. Hindenburg and Ludendorff demanded his ouster; the kaiser gave way and Germany passed over completely to a military dictatorship.

As the political structure crumbled, power ran amok. Military ambition lost all restraint. Germany was to stretch through the Ukraine to the Caucasus and Georgia. *Ostraum* was to supplement *Mitteleuropa*. By the end, Germany's growing appetite brought conflict with the Austrians and even with the Turks. Illustrations abound of the heavy-handed clumsiness of German diplomacy. The military seemed incapable of sustaining any genuine relationship with independent allies. Increasingly absent from German calculations was any conception of a general balance, or of the necessity for leaving other countries some acceptable role and situation in the interests of long-range peace. Europe was to be treated by the Germans as India or Africa had been by the British.

It is extraordinary how these ambitions continued to grow right until August 1918. Thoughts of compromise were firmly repulsed as traitorous. Yet all was fantasy. The real war was hopeless. Army leaders presumably knew, but deceived everyone. Even the kaiser was astonished at the end. Suddenly, the military declared the war lost. The emperor was dispatched and the civilians summoned back to bear the onus of defeat.

Germany's "Guilt" Reconsidered

What can we learn from studying Germany's aims in the First World War? Were the Germans "guilty" of starting the war? Did they reveal an insatiable aggressiveness against their neighbors? Is there a direct continuity between Bethmann-Hollweg's aggression and that of Hitler?

Certainly the Germans bore a heavy responsibility for turning the immediate Balkan Crisis into a general war. For economic and especially military reasons, the Germans felt desperate. A general war might have started at any time over the Balkans; the Germans wanted it earlier rather than later. Bethmann gambled on a decisive diplomatic victory without a general war, but was ready for war if it came. In short, he was not innocent of the consequences. Neither, it may be said, was Austria, Russia, France, or Britain.

The quarrel among the European powers was not just over the Balkans. The whole thrust of Germany's development almost inevitably threatened the traditional European balance of power. By Bethmann's era that thrust had become a conscious ambition to make Germany dominant on the Continent and a major power in the world. Only thus, Germans reasoned, could their extraordinary growth not be strangled by the limits of their geopolitical situation. The existing European balance, they believed, was a false balance, sustained by Britain to keep the European states from competing with it for empire. Only if France and Russia were defeated decisively, and Germany liberated from encirclement, could a genuine world balance form itself around the surviving superpowers – Germany, the United States, Great Britain, and someday others, most probably China.

Those who had themselves carved up Africa and Asia were of course outraged that something similar should be proposed in Europe. But the Germans could claim that the creation of the great extra-European states and colonial empires demanded a comparable recasting of Europe. That necessity, moreover, was not Germany's fault. It was not the Germans who had made the balance of 1815 obsolete. They had not been the first to develop the dynamic power of modern industry. They were, in fact, the last to form a nation-state, the last to seek an empire.

These general geopolitical perspectives were the staple substance of German middle-class opinion, a major part of the ideology by which the bourgeois parties reached out to mobilize a mass electorate. They were widely shared among German industrialists, politicians, intellectuals, and military and civilian officials. In short, the Germans were certainly "aggressive" against the status quo and this "guilt" spread throughout the society. In particular, as so many scholars have been at such pains to point out, no significant difference over these ultimate aims separated "moderate" civilians, like Bethmann-Hollweg, from the military chieftains and annexationist politicians.

But if these ultimate hegemonic aims were widely shared, notions of the actual European structure to result varied sharply, as did the methods envisaged for realizing it. What Bethmann hoped the natural weight of a dynamic Germany could achieve through diplomacy or limited war, and sustain by indirect pressures and inducements, the political generals led by Ludendorff expected to wrest by the sword and sustain by uncompromising force. As the hopeless war continued, Ludendorff and the annexationists increasingly gained the upper hand, a development as counterproductive as it was deplorable. By the end, they were planning a Germany stretching from the Caucasus to the Channel. Whatever the theoretical merits of their geopolitical case, the Germans' lack of self-restraint in pursuing their goals worked strongly to their disadvantage. Thanks to annexationist fever, the war's original defensive rationale was lost. Germany grew increasingly isolated. Attempts to win and hold allies formed a remarkable string of failures. No grand cosmopolitan conceptions softened or legitimized German pretensions. No imaginative European scheme sought to appease neighboring interests or give dignity to their decline. Instead, a brutal and heavy-handed manner produced resistance to arrangements that, under more genial masters, might have appeared bearable and perhaps inevitable. It is not difficult, of course, to find parallels in this unrestrained use of force – the Belgians in the Congo, the British in Ireland or India, the French in Morocco, the Russians throughout Asia. Still, in the twentieth century to apply such naked power to other European states was deeply shocking. It seemed a barbaric reversion after a century of progress toward a more secure civilization.

How could the Germans, who had been mainstays of nineteeth-century civilization, and who had so richly shared in its progress, turn themselves into the "Huns" of the modern era? Perhaps, as A. J. P. Taylor once suggested, their racist view of the neighboring Slavs nourished a characteristic brutality in dealing with all people unlike themselves. Perhaps. But Taylor's explanation seems too partisan and partial. Why were the British not similarly poisoned by their treatment of the Irish and Indians, or the Americans by their treatment of Indians, Mexicans, or blacks?

That poet of German historians, Ludwig Dehio, provides a richer and more comprehensive view. Germany's behavior in the First War, he argued, was characteristic of all

those who had pretended to continental hegemony –
Charles V, Philip II, Louis XIV, Napoleon I:

At the beginning of the struggle the supreme power reaches the culmination of its previous history, and its initial successes form a mag-
nificent, triumphant, clear-cut crystalization of its nature. But as the
struggle drags wearily on, intense euphoria turns into daemonic excess.
The screws are turned too tight. Finally, the rulers, like gamblers with
no real understanding of the game they are playing, stake their fundamental material and moral values. Their hopes flared up until the last
moment, only to lure them on to their ultimate fall.[5]

[For Germany] all the heights and all the depths were touched, not in
the course of decades but in a matter of years. In 1914, confronted with
the hatred of "a whole world of enemies," we experienced the intoxicat-
ing intensification of our whole being; but this sudden spiritual isolation, which was the result of our political isolation, contained the seeds
of excess. This development . . . was hastened by the accumulated
emotions of the majority. It shattered the spiritual balance of the
nation. Encircled by hatred, the people replied with its own hatred.
Society and the machinery of the state were overstrained by the lonely
and glorious, but ill-fated struggle, and traditions were distorted. Ex-
tremist and monomaniac ideas, which might have remained mere
marginal phenomena in a calmer context, began to spread.[6]

Even Dehio, however, cannot resist claiming a greater
wickedness for the Germans than they deserve. With all
their fears and frustrations in 1914, were the Germans any
more warlike or ambitious than the other Great Powers?
Indeed, as Taylor notes about his own country:

There were plenty of warmongers in England before 1914, and military and naval influences were as strong as in Germany, if not stronger.
Fischer's display of German war aims during the First World War
looks decisive until you turn to British war aims, as demonstrated by
Roger Louis in Africa. . . . The British, too, were out for World Power,
and their aims were, if anything, more far-reaching than those of the
Germans.

[5] Ludwig Dehio, Germany and World Politics in the Twentieth Century (New
York: Knopf, 1959), p. 18.
[6] Ibid., p. 19.

I agree that the German government gave the formal push to war in 1914, but the push was widely welcomed in England and France.[7]

Imperial and Nazi Germanies: Continuity or Catastrophe?

Bismarck's Reich was, in due course, succeeded by Hitler's. The madness of the late empire was only a prelude. Hitler not only took up the broad imperial war aims, but in their most brutal annexationist form. The worst characteristics of Imperial Germany were, in due course, exhibited to a lunatic degree. After Hitler, it was only natural to assume that Germans had had the same goals all along and had been incapable of achieving them in any other way.

The broad question of Hitler's continuity in German history will have to wait until the chapters that deal with him specifically. One point, however, seems appropriate to make here. Bethmann-Hollweg, whatever his mistakes, was a very different type from Hitler. He was also a very different type from the annexationists, or from the military leaders like Ludendorff or Tirpitz. Were these differences purely personal or was there a rational and humane form of German hegemony that Bethmann represented?

Despite the great scholarly energy that attempts to prove the contrary, it seems perverse to deny the fundamental difference in the quality of the hegemony envisioned by Bethmann, on the one hand, and by the annexationists and Nazis on the other. Bethmann's quarrel with the annexationists arose not merely because he was relatively "soft" or humane, or more sophisticated about wielding power efficiently, but because, unlike Ludendorff, he was a conservative rather than an adventurer. Bethmann sprang from a settled order whose stability depended upon a prin-

---

[7] A. J. P. Taylor, "Fritz Fischer and his School," *Journal of Modern History*, vol. 47, no. 1 (1975), p. 123.

cipled consensus and whose survival required intelligent adaptation to a modernizing world. Ludendorff and Tirpitz, by contrast, were not conservatives but rootless adventurers – Nietzschean technocrats – who in the name of progress and modernity brought the ruin that unhinged a whole society.

Both types are common enough in our modern era. In Imperial Germany perhaps the contrast and confrontation was exceptionally sharp. Few countries combined such powerful conservative traditions with so pervasive a sense of limitless Faustian power. Few, of course, had transformed themselves so rapidly into modern states. Bethmann's demise represented the defeat of conservatism and the victory of adventure.

The defeat marked the end of rational government in wartime Germany. Unlike the French or British parliamentary systems, Germany's imperial constitution, with its conservative technocratic executive, proved unable to stand the strain of all-out war. What were the reasons? Part of the explanation may be personal. Bethmann-Hollweg, unlike Clemenceau or Lloyd George, lacked the demonic power to master the wild forces called up by the war and keep them yoked to a rational state policy. He was too inhibited a personality, too respectful of tradition to be able to preserve it. Bethmann is also often criticized for not being democratic enough. Had he brought party leaders more into his confidence, it is said, he could have built the Reichstag into an independent base to check the military. But the case is hardly self-evident. Bethmann himself found the party leaders an unpromising lot, habituated to the restless intrigues of interest politics and undisciplined parliamentarism. The National Liberals, for example, were intransigent annexationists and missed every chance to convert themselves from a class pressure group into a genuine governing party. Beyond the parties lay the interests, in particular the blind greed of big industry. Nor was the educated public a promising base for support. Despite a fashionable tendency to lay all of Germany's follies to atavistic Junkers, or an authoritarian political system, the German bourgeoisie must share a good part of the blame, in particular their intellectual leaders – the university professors and the Protestant clergy. German academic luminaries, for example, cheered on the virulent annexationist societies. Small wonder that after a decade or two of pervasive imperialist propaganda, the German public had itself become highly adventurous.

After his fall, Bethmann, even while admitting the particular mistakes of German policy, was himself inclined to stress the warlike thrust of mass opinion. A private letter to Prince Max of Baden, dated January 17, 1918, sums up his view:

Imperialism, nationalism and economic materialism, which in broad outline have governed the policies of all nations during the past generation, set themselves goals that could be pursued by each nation only at the cost of a general collision. It is true that besides these general reasons there were special circumstances that militated in favour of war, including those in which Germany in 1870–71 entered the circle of Great Powers, subsequently achieved world stature and became the object of vengeful envy on the part of the other Great Powers, largely though not entirely by her own fault. Both of these lines, however, the general and the special, are so closely interlinked that it is impossible to say on which side lay the more powerful driving force. For myself, I see the general constellation [of public opinion] as the crucial element. How else explain the senseless and impassioned zeal which allowed countries like, Italy, Rumania and even America, not originally involved in the war, no rest until they too had immersed themselves in the bloodbath? Surely this is the immediate, tangible expression of a general disposition towards war in the world.[8]

Bethmann was doubtless right to stress the universality of this popular bent for war. No one who studies the social and cultural history of the various Western countries can

[8] H.W. Koch, *The Origins of the First World War: Great Power Rivalry and German War Aims* (London: Macmillan, 1972), pp. 251–2.

help but feel the mounting tensions of the prewar decade and the widespread relief brought by the war's outbreak. Once those in charge of policy maneuvered themselves into a general breakdown, the forces released wreaked wanton destruction in all directions; they proved impossible to control until exhausted by war, and, in many places, by revolution as well. Rational government was everywhere maintained with difficulty.

If the breakdown seems more extreme in Germany than in Britain or France, it must not be forgotten that the Western Allies were winning and the Gemans losing. Bethmann's position became hopeless as Germany's position became hopeless. His only policy was negotiation and, perhaps unfortunately for all, no one on the other side was seriously interested. Once Germany had been foolish enough to provoke a war it could not win, Bismarck's nightmare became a reality. The Allied coalition was determined to crush the German challenge. Under the circumstances, the collapse of rational policy in Germany seems more an effect of defeat than a cause.

The reasons for this Allied determination, of course, lead back to our original theme. Germany's "aggression" was not so much unique in its intensity as in its inconvenience. The rise of Bismarck's creation meant shattering Europe's traditional balance and upsetting the world's arrangements in general. In the end, Germany could not sustain its challenge. Bismarck's successors could not win the game that he had started. Perhaps they lacked his skill. Perhaps, too, he had not left them a very good hand.

4

Germany's Imperial Economy

Introduction: The German Economy and the
German Problem

As the two preceding chapters indicate, economic considerations strongly affected Imperial German policy. The Great
Depression led Bismarck to protectionism and a new conservative coalition in the empire, while it hastened the
unraveling of his alliance diplomacy in Europe. Fears and
hopes for Germany's economic development were an inte-
gral part of those broader geopolitical perspectives that
guided German policy into the First World War. In short,
even if traditional history has often neglected economic
factors, their close interprenetration with general domestic
and foreign policies is evident.

Some historians carry the point further. A distinguished German school of broad Marxist persuasion, which
also owes much to Schumpeter, finds in Germany's economic formation the very key to the German problem.
Hans-Ulrich Wehler, for example, argues that Bismarck's
opting for state intervention in the economic and social

fields made the years from 1879 to 1885, in effect, a second "founding period" for the Reich. As Wehler sees it, Bismarck, to reconcile his authoritarian regime with a reactionary society, an advanced capitalism, and a depression, fixed Germany on a course of imperialist expansionism abroad and reactionary politics at home. Protectionism and imperialism furnished the means both for a countercyclical policy to mitigate the crisis of overproduction and for the continual legitimizing of his authoritarian regime. That regime had behind it a reactionary social coalition. Big agriculture and heavy industry were united to expand Germany abroad and block democracy at home. Wehler is preoccupied with his own country's internal development and not much interested in comparisons with other nations. As I read him, he is not trying to prove Germany more "imperialist" than Britain, France, or the United States. In any event, if colonial wars and possessions are any indicators, he would not find it easy to do so. A. J. P. Taylor's *Course of German History,* by contrast, suggests a uniquely power-oriented and aggressive quality to Germany's economic formation. German economic development is said to have shown an exceptional mercantilist bent toward domestic concentration and aggressive foreign trading. In effect, the German model was inspired not by the peaceful liberalism of Cobden, but by the armed mercantilism of Clausewitz. Like the old Prussian state, the German economy was scientifically organized for combat. Trade was war by other means.

Taylor's *Course of German History* demonstrates the view with customary *brio*:

The tariff of 1879 was not created to protect new struggling industries from established British competition – the colonial tariff pattern. Nor was it invoked, as in France, to save leisurely old-fashioned industries from the challenge of the up-to-date. German industry was the most modern and best established in Europe. The tariffs gave protection in the way that bombing aeroplanes give defence. They were a weapon of war: to destroy competitors by dumping, and, ultimately, to enroll consumers by compulsion.[1]

As a consequence, Taylor concludes, Imperial Germany became an unstable maverick in the world economy: "German industry grew ever more top-heavy and the need for new outlets ever more pressing."[2] Protection endowed Germany with a dynamic but unbalanced economy that ultimately could only be sustained by the conquest of Europe. The instability of Bismarck's Reich in the world political system was thus matched and reinforced by its instability in the world economy.

Integrating Imperial Germany's economic and social development with its politics obviously gives a far richer and more comprehensive view of each. Some of the fashionable conclusions, however, seem somewhat overdrawn. From the perspective of an economic liberal, Germany's industrial development doubtless seems deplorable. But Germany's economic formation was not so unusual. I suspect German "mercantilism" was less the product of a unique German political culture than of the evolving nature of modern industry. Similarly, while a present-day liberal or Marxist may find the social system, political structure, and general style of the imperial regime repugnant, I wonder if Imperial Germany's political system was, in truth, so radically different from those of Britain and France. In all three countries, the gentry and upper middle classes were coalescing to defend their privileges, workers were suppressed, governments were high-handed when they could get away with it, and militarism and imperialism were rampant. Moreover, I do not find an altogether convincing link between Imperial Germany's foreign conflicts and the supposedly illiberal features of its political regime and economy. In any event, the presumably liberal powers,

[1] A. J. P. Taylor, *The Course of German History* (London: Hamilton, 1945), p. 126.
[2] Ibid.

like Britain and the United States, were hardly less aggressive in their foreign economic relations.

The rest of this chapter considers some of these issues further. The first part discusses Germany's economic formation and its consequences for Germany's international role. The second examines some of the broad theories linking Imperial Germany's political-economic character and its "aggression" in the First World War.

Germany's Late Development

What was so special about the German economy? One difference stands out above all. Compared to Britain, France, Belgium, or even the United States, Germany's economic growth came very late and very fast. Perhaps it is best to consider a brief historical survey of its development.

In 1850, Germany was overwhelmingly agricultural, with relatively undeveloped industry and commerce and no highly developed urban centers. As late as 1871, roughly two-thirds of Prussia's population was rural, a proportion that had barely changed over the preceding half century. Between 1871 and 1901, by contrast, rural population in Germany as a whole dropped from 64 to 40 percent. Big towns grew fastest.

Germany's arrested development had numerous causes. In the sixteenth century, the diversion of world trade to the Atlantic route brought decline to Germany's once-flourishing commerce. In the seventeenth century, religious and political struggles, exacerbated by outside interventions, culminated in the appallingly destructive Thirty Years' War. The war completed the eclipse of the middle classes. The treaty of Westphalia hampered trade by cementing the country's division into numerous states. Within most of these states, princely absolutism reigned supreme. Agriculture dominated economic life. Parts of Germany were actually more "feudal" in the eighteenth century than in the sixteenth. After 1648, for example, some areas saw serfdom installed for the first time. Crafts were dominated by guilds, and large-scale enterprise of any sort was difficult and rare.

For many German states, not until the French Revolution and its Napoleonic aftermath was there any great impulse to change. French imperialism provoked not only German nationalism but, in Prussia notably, an indigenous reforming liberalism. The subsequent collapse of the French imperium demanded a major political reconstruction which, however conservative its purpose, fostered a strong predisposition for rational reform, in the Prussian bureaucracy particularly. Prussia established a system of primary education that was the envy of Europe. Manorial restrictions were formally ended, even if the peasantry was only slowly emancipated from eastern estates. By 1834, Prussia had maneuvered the German states into the *Zollverein*, a customs union that liberalized inner German trade and oriented it away from Austria's continental embrace. It was a direction that suited both Prussia's Junker gentry, interested in exporting their grain, and the country's major commercial interests, oriented toward the sea rather than overland toward the south.

For a variety of reasons, German economic life finally began to stir in the 1830s. The population was rising rapidly, which encouraged agriculturalists to develop new lands and plant new crops, especially potatoes and sugar beets. Meanwhile, the foundations of industrialization were falling into place. Government reforms in Prussia and several other states provided an exceptionally high level of general education; subsidies fostered outstanding technical research; and regulations supported exacting standards of craftsmanship.

Except in Silesia, the Prussian state had not taken an active role in fostering industry directly; but in the 1830s it began to promote telegraph, railway, and canal building. By the late 1840s, railway building, about half promoted directly by the state, grew intense and provoked a series of economic booms and crashes as well as a startling increase in foreign trade.

From 1850 to 1914, German economic development divided itself roughly into three phases: 1850 to 1873 was a period of high growth, especially important for changes in technology and organization; 1874 to 1895 was a prolonged period of relative stagnation; 1896 to 1913 was once again a period of accelerated growth. The causes of these cyclical shifts were, as always, multiple and complex. Perhaps the most obvious correlations were with the gold discoveries in 1848 and 1886, which sent waves of stimulation throughout the world economy. The relative stagnation in the century's last quarter was, of course, part of the worldwide Great Depression. Whatever the causes of these cyclical swings, they were critical to Germany's political-economic development. The Great Depression promoted Bismarck's shift to protectionism in 1879, and the general German predilection for concentration and cartels.

However uneven, German economic growth was astonishing by earlier standards. From 1850 to 1913 the net domestic product increased at an average rate of 2.6 percent per annum. Domestic production in 1913 was thus five times greater than in 1850 – two and a half times greater per capita. Most Germans enjoyed a sharp rise in their standard of living; real industrial wages actually doubled between 1871 and 1913.

Figures for particular industries are, of course, even more spectacular. Coal production jumped from 29.4 million metric tons in 1871 to 191.5 millions in 1913. Only Britain rivaled Germany in this sphere. By 1910, Germany had surpassed Britain in iron and steel production, as the following tabulation in millions of tons shows:

	Pig Iron	Steel
United Kingdom	10.2	7.6
Germany	14.8	13.1

German machine building grew at a dizzy rate, as employment figures indicate:

1861:   51,000
1882:   356,000
1907:   1,120,000

Economic success was particularly striking in three later-developing industries: chemicals, electricity, and optics. In both chemical and electrical industries, the Germans had come from far behind to challenge other national industries – the Americans in electricity and the British in chemicals. By 1907, Siemens and AEG the leading electrical firms – employed 142,000 people between them. Half the international trade in electrical products was of German origin. By the same period, the German chemical industry employed 270,000 people and produced 90 percent of the world's industrial dyes. These new industries were particularly impressive illustrations of the German capacity for large-scale industrial organization. Each industry was dominated by a few giant firms closely linked with the big banks. All depended heavily upon high technology and foreign trade, the former nurtured through close links with universities and research institutes, the latter served by a well-organized commercial and diplomatic network. As the British economic historian Clapham observed in 1921, "[Germany's] great companies were international powers, with extensive diplomatic influence and unstinted support from Government."

The German economy also, in fact, sheltered innumerable small banks, industries, cooperatives, and craft enterprises. But the giant firms in steelmaking and the newer technological industries were the most distinctive part of German economic development, particularly by comparison with Britain or France. Giant enterprises were greatly facilitated by Germany's company law, which managed to impose rational structure and strict accounting without interfering with concentration. Cartels, too, were deliberately fostered by legislation making their agreements legally enforceable.

The German capacity for large-scale organization was tied closely to the special nature of German banks. By 1870, joint-stock banks were becoming the focal points in organizing Germany's industrial development. Whereas the British retained a sharp distinction between clearing and investment or "merchant" banking, the Germans developed "universal" banks, designed to convert every conceivable type of fund into capital. The banks themselves took over many of the traditional functions of money and stock markets. In the giant industrial enterprises, Germany's big banks were frequently the largest shareholders and providers of capital, the catalysts for organizing amalgamations and cartels, as well as major promoters of exports and business interests abroad.

This concentration of investment capital and lack of a capital market along British or French lines showed in the relatively low rate of German investment abroad. The big banks were relatively uninterested in foreign investment, unless tied to the trading interests of domestic companies. Thus, for example, while 77 percent of all new securities sold in France in 1911 were for foreign enterprise, the corresponding figure for Germany was 11 percent. With their bounding growth, the Germans were generally relatively short of capital. But thanks in part to a financial structure that prompted a comprehensive view of national economic development, what capital the Germans did have was channeled. into domestic industrial development rather than foreign lending.

Germany's relative indifference to foreign investment did not extend to trade. As might have been expected, German trade grew by leaps and bounds. Between 1887 and 1912, German imports roughly trebled. Germany became the largest importer of raw materials among the

European states. German importing had been slowly shifting its direction toward "world" sources, the United States
and Latin America in particular. Nevertheless, by 1914
Europe still remained the preponderant source.

German export promotion was not only highly successful,
but was thought exceptionally aggressive. Roughly 80 percent of Germany's exports went to the rest of Europe.
Thanks to the intimate ties between banks and industries,
and the banks' active role in export promotion, German
financing was generally extremely generous – to the frequent astonishment and dismay of its competition.

Germany's trade balance, nevertheless, turned unfavor-
ble in the 1890s, a normal development among Europe's
advanced industrial countries in this period. In any event,
Germany's rising income from "invisibles," in particular
shipping, more than offset its trade deficit. Germany's merchant marine was highly modern and surpassed only by
Britain's in tonnage.

Germany's trade deficit was intimately linked with the
fate of its agriculture. Despite spectacular industrialization, agriculture remained extremely important to both
the economy and society. Indeed, at the foundation of the
empire in 1871, Germany could still, according to Clapham, be described as a country of free landowning peas-
ants and powerful cultivating squires. The type of agriculture varied from "big peasant" holdings in Bavaria and
Mecklenberg, to smaller holdings characteristic of the
Rhineland, to the big estates of the east. The big landowners typically held 2,000 acres, which they managed themselves. Roughly one-quarter of the empire's agricultural
land was in such estates, a proportion that was slowly
declining by the 1900s. As was common everywhere in
industrializing Europe, the proportion of labor in agriculture was gradually falling. Still, not until the 1890s did
manufacturing employ more male workers than agriculture and agriculture, forestry, and fishing remained a

major sector of employment thereafter, particularly for women. In 1907, for example, families directly connected with agriculture and forestry constituted 28.6 percent of the population.

German agriculture, moreover, was no exception to the rapid progress that characterized the rest of the economy. By the 1840s and 1850s, the German farmers, especially the Junkers, were among the finest in Europe. Agricultural productivity and output continued to expand thereafter. Thanks to the potato and the sugar beet, Germany remained without an overall agricultural deficit and was even a net exporter. Between 1890 and 1900, for example, sugar made up 6 percent of German exports – exceeding coal, iron, or machinery. Pork production also increased rapidly. In the 1890s, German agriculture went through a remarkable period of technological progress, a steady growth of yields led by the big estates. Germans were pioneers in the development and use of fertilizers, in particular of phosphate fertilizer, a by-product of the Thomas-Gilchrist process of iron smelting. Farm mechanization proceeded apace after 1900. Despite its impressive efforts, however, German agricultural production was steadily losing ground before the needs of the exploding population, even with the protection that came in the late 1870s and again after 1902. By 1910, 40 percent of all wheat and 15 percent of all grain had to be imported. The tariffs favoring Junker grain producers undoubtedly helped slow down the contraction of agriculture and its revenues, but also delayed structural adaptations and an upgraded output. Thus, even if Germany was 95 percent self-sufficient in terms of calories and vegetable foodstuffs in 1913, its agriculture might have been more efficient had it concentrated less on grain and more on animal raising.

The problems of German grain farming, however, had nothing to do with efficiency in a technical sense. German yields were far higher than those of her more "efficient" competitors, as Tables 1 and 2, taken from a contemporary source, make clear.

Nevertheless, as international transportation became easy and cheap, German land and labor were too expensive to compete against the products of the abundant and perhaps badly exploited farmlands of Russia and the United States. British agriculture, of course, had faced the same situation. The British solution – theoretically in 1846 and actually in the 1880s had been to sacrifice domestic agriculture. Comparative advantage decreed that Britain's capital and labor should devote itself to industry and commerce. Britain's population would be fed from cheap imported food. British agriculturalists, despite their continuing political power, wealth, and social prestige, had not been able to marshal a victorious coalition for protection. Bourgeois interests triumphed over the gentry. Germany, as we know, followed a different path. With Bismarck's tariffs, the Junkers, as well as a large segment of industry, refused to accept the logic of comparative advantage. For

Table 1. *Aggregate yield of crops in various countries, 1911–13 (in millions of tons)*

Harvest year		Wheat & rye	Barley	Oats	Potatoes
1912	Germany	15.9	3.5	8.5	50.2
1912	Russia	42.6	9.9	14.1	36.9
1912	Austria-Hungary	11.2	3.3	3.6	18.5
1911	France	10.4	1.1	5.1	11.5
1912	Canada	5.4	0.9	5.6	2.2
1912	United States	20.8	4.9	20.6	11.4
1912/13	Argentina	6.4	—	1.7	—
1911/12	British India	8.4	—	—	—

Source: Karl Helfferich, *Germany's Economic Progress and National Wealth, 1888–1913* (New York: Germanistic Society of America, 1914), p. 55.

them, the logic of power was meant to dominate the logic of the market.

How were the Junkers strong enough to impose agricultural protection upon the German bourgeois commercial and industrial interests? Their success depended upon that conjuncture of unfavorable economic developments discussed in the preceding chapter. As the world economy went into a general decline after 1873, Germany industry, particularly coal, iron, and steel, whose growth in the early seventies had been extremely rapid, faced a desperate crisis of overproduction. Thus these industries were already militantly disposed to protectionism. By the end of the 1870s, German agriculture, traditionally devoted to free trade, began to be hurt by the cheap foreign imports. Thus Bismarck's protectionist alliance of "rye and iron" in 1879.

As discussed in Chapter 2, Bismarck had ample motive

Table 2. *Yield of crops per hectare in various countries, 1911–13 (in metric cwt)*

Harvest year		Wheat	Rye	Barley	Oats	Potatoes
1912	Germany	22.6	18.5	21.9	19.4	150.3
1912	Russia	6.9	9.0	8.7	8.5	81.7
1912	Austria-Hungary	⎰ 15.0	14.6	16.0	13.0	100.2
		⎱ 12.7	11.6	13.9	10.4	84.4
1911	France	13.8	14.3	14.3	12.6	74.2
1912	Canada	13.7	12.0	16.7	15.0	115.8
1912	United States	10.7	10.6	16.0	13.4	76.2
1912/13	Argentina	9.3	—	—	14.1	—
1911/12	British India	8.7	—	—	—	—

Note: 1 metric cwt = 220 lbs.
Source: Karl Helfferich, *Germany's Economic Progress and National Wealth, 1888–1913* (New York: Germanistic Society of America, 1914), p. 55.

for his protectionist policy. The empire had been born in a great surge of industrialization and prosperity. The legitimacy of its upstart regime was bound up with being able to sustain that industrial prosperity. The depression was thus a great political as well as economic and social danger. Constitutional and monetary restrictions made manipulation of industrial trade through protection and dumping the most effective countercyclical policy available. As for "rye," Bismarck, himself a Junker and big farmer, was doubtless sympathetic to the economic interests of agriculture and not inclined to underestimate the importance of Prussia's gentry to its army and state. In any event, their political leverage was formidable. Thanks to the weighted franchise, agrarian interests remained predominant in the old Prussian Landtag, and thus exercised a legislative veto in Prussia, the federal Reich's dominant state.

Beyond class interest, geopolitical arguments for agricultural protectionism lay easily to hand. German fears of a food and general trade deficit were not so much commercial as political and military. Whereas purely economic considerations might have justified Germany in following Britain's example and growing ever more dependent upon foreign food, Germany's geopolitical position was thought to be radically different. Britain was an island with a huge empire and a fleet that dominated the seas. Germany had neither a serious empire nor, as yet, a rival fleet. Germany's geographical position made blockading its world commerce relatively easy. Germany, moreover, was surrounded by two great and increasingly hostile continental powers – Russia and France. Both were more self-sufficient in food and both had other resources: Russia had vast supplies of domestic raw materials; France had more secure access to foreign suppliers. Hence, the obvious conclusion, so welcome to its governing elites: Germany would have to protect agriculture and strive for self-sufficiency.

Beyond these military arguments, German protectionism, agricultural and industrial, was only the natural expression in the international sphere of the characteristic evolution of the German economy domestically. For power, self-consciously employed, did play a major role in developing German industry and commerce. It was not merely that the state, through tariffs, legislation, subsidies, specialized technical education and regulation generally, played a more considerable part in forming the economy than in Britain. But within the business world itself, power engendered by large-scale organization had far more to do with shaping German industry and commerce than in more market-oriented systems, like Britain or even France. The trend toward monopolistic giant enterprises, which also characterized the United States, was at least resisted by the American government. The German government encouraged it.

In consequence, it is often noted, the belated but spectacular rise of industry and commerce in Germany lacked some of the main accompanying political and cultural effects prevalent elsewhere, especially in Britain. The liberal ideals of free trade and a market economy never came to dominate the political culture. Imperial Germany was "outward looking" but not liberal. Germany's "modernization" came at a later stage of industrial development. Put crudely, the German bourgeoisie were less the independent-minded entrepreneurs, tinkerers, and traders of British capitalism; they were the "organization men" of a later capitalism. Their capacity for large-scale and rationalized organization was, of course, not unconnected with Germany's economic growth and commercial success abroad, nor with the resentment and fear that the country's progress aroused among its neighbors.

To the Germans, of course, concentration — far from being a blemish — seemed inseparable from progress toward a more rational economy. Large integrated enterprises were seen as the way of the future — the best means not only to promote competitiveness abroad, but also to avoid those economic shocks that wasted capital and disrupted the social and political fabric at home. Britain's liberalism, with its free market booms and busts, seemed a more primitive capitalism. It wasted national resources, and brought insecurity to the middle classes and misery to the poor. Germany's was a more modern and rational system, a model widely admired in both Britain and the United States.

In this context, the other main element of Bismarck's protectionism, namely the extraordinary system of social insurance for workers, should not be forgotten. Here, too, politically organized power was used to control the economic environment rather than to allow state and society to be victimized by it. Indeed, many who stress the autocratic and conservative character of Imperial German policy do not weigh sufficiently the real progress toward social security and integration achieved by that regime – particularly in contrast with more "liberal" Britain. Public education, for example, was nearly universal in Germany, and had been so since the early nineteenth century. In Britain, by contrast, as late as 1860, at best roughly half the children of school age were actually in school. Improvement over the rest of the century in the extent and quality of British mass education cannot be described as rapid. The significance of such fundamental policies and attitudes for the mobility and integration of a society is as obvious as it is overwhelming. Nor are such basic social facts irrelevant in explaining Germany's superior capacity for achieving large-scale industrial organization.

This observation leads back to the questions raised at the outset of this chapter. Contemporary liberal or Marxist analysts often tend to find Imperial Germany's predilection for giant industry and mercantilism a peculiarly sinister national characteristic. Such judgments seem hasty and unbalanced. Germany's economic growth, after all, came not in the age of textiles, but in the age of steel and the newer science-based industries like chemicals, optics, and electricity. In such industries, large-scale organization, encompassing the steady development and application of science and technology, was often the key to success. The Germans and Americans, both of whom came to industrialization later than Britain, France, or Belgium, pioneered these new forms of large-scale organization. And they were more efficient for the newer industries, in fact, than the smaller, more market-oriented firms of earlier capitalism. Insofar as the other older industrial economies could not adopt the new forms, they declined. Where they did succeed in the new industries, as, for example, the British in chemicals, they adopted big structures similar to those in Germany and the United States. Those firms displaced in their markets by more efficient German competition were, of course, unlikely to be pleased. Liberal market principles provided, no doubt, a comforting ideology. But for the new industries, with their enormous outlays of capital, the pure market of which economists dream was an unrealistic and wasteful system for managing supply and demand.

The Great Depression, of course, hastened the trend toward public and private mercantilism. All states, in their fashion, became increasingly involved in managing their economies – through tariffs and other trade regulations as well as in the imperialist search for secure markets and sources of supply. Even the British, if they remained formally liberal, nevertheless tended increasingly to retreat to their privileged overseas markets.

As the world evolved toward an outward-thrusting aggressive mercantilism, competition inevitably became fierce. In a world whose expectations of endless growth and facile competition had been rudely disappointed by a long depression, Darwinian ideas inevitably came to permeate the general perspectives of businessmen, politicians, and the general public. With political power so involved, competition was almost fated to turn into conflict. To say that the Germans were uniquely aggressive in such a context is perhaps only to say that they were unusually successful.

German Economic Development and the First World War

For the past half century, analysts have sought to find a close connection between political and economic development in industrial societies and the causes of the First World War. Roughly speaking, these analysts form two broad schools – those influenced by Marx and those influenced by Schumpeter. The first group blames capitalism in general; the second, Germany in particular.

Classic Marxists, like Lenin and Luxemburg, based their historical theories of imperialist conflict primarily upon an interpretation of German economic development before the First World War. As they saw it, capitalist economies, relentlessly centralized by banks, were plagued by a surplus of productive capacity and investment capital. To avoid collapse, their states pursued aggressive foreign policies designed to ensure adequate markets and investment opportunities. The relationship of these powerful, dynamic, but unstable national economic systems grew increasingly Darwinian. War was natural among them. As later analysts have increasingly emphasized, armaments expenditures became, in themselves, an essential device to mitigate overproduction.

Both Lenin and Luxemburg, although they focused on Germany, regarded their analysis as valid for all advanced capitalist societies. In general, Marxist analysis blames the world war not so much on Germany as on capitalism. Germany was late to develop and hence its imperial impulse came after the others had picked off the choice spoils. But Germany's "aggression" was no worse than that which had earlier led British and French capitalism to penetrate and often to annex large parts of the world. Hence, the German Problem was intrinsically no worse than the British or French.

Schumpeter and his followers have produced a rather more selective condemnation. Schumpeter, paralleling somewhat an analysis developed by Veblen, linked Germany's aggressive external policies to its peculiar combination of industrial modernization, authoritarian politics, and reactionary society. In this view, Germany's problem was less its thrusting capitalists than its beleaguered Junkers. Germany's late economic development left its bourgeoisie economically preoccupied and politically diffident. Hence the feudal Junker elite continued to dominate German society and politics. But the agricultural economic base of this ruling class was in fatal decline. To avoid extinction within a modernizing society, the Junkers took to war, their class specialty. In both their militarism and their demagogic mass politics, they combined the latest technology with atavistic ideals. Hence, Germany's aggressiveness could be traced not to the rise of capitalism, but to the perpetuation of an obsolescent precapitalist class, and its values, within a modernizing society.

Schumpeter's view received powerful reinforcement from the economist Alexander Gerschenkron's *Bread and Democracy*, written during the Second World War. And it is prominently reflected in several important recent German interpretations. All give a decisive significance to Bismarck's original protectionist coalition of heavy industry and agrarians, militantly reaffirmed by Bülow in the tariff controversies of 1902. Tariffs, in this view, were the issue around which a reactionary government perpetuated both itself and an obsolescent social structure. In return for tariff concessions to overextended heavy industry, the Junker farmers protected their economic base and retained the political and social hegemony that had been theirs since 1867. The big capitalists were supposedly contented with this German version of the Victorian Compromise because industry's economic power was growing and its interests were sufficiently protected by direct contacts with the emperor and bureaucracy. Those industrialists with social ambitions could easily buy mortgaged estates, become landowners, be received at court, and get army reserve commissions for their sons.

A more detailed analysis reveals, of course, significant divisions among the bourgeoisie. Burgeoning commercial interests gave rise to the antiprotectionist *Hansabund* in 1902; newer, lighter industries, like electrical goods, also tended to oppose the tariffs. But the return to general prosperity in the late nineties, it is explained, appeased even the disaffected, including labor, whose real wages were rising rapidly. To be sure, socialists despised Junkerdom and many liberals wanted an end to Prussia's anachronistic franchise. But the bulk of liberal bourgeois opinion was being systematically deflected into imperialism. Spurred on by Pan-German associations, or the new Navy League, the middle classes turned from their domestic political aspirations to a militarist and aggressive identification with foreign affairs. In any event, the bulk of the middle classes, the intelligentsia included, were proudly nationalist and grateful to the Junker army for giving the Reich its unity. Germans thought themselves, on the whole, to have a better political, economic, and social system than the French, British, or Russians. Hence, only the Social Democrats strongly opposed the conservative political bloc and its policy. And even the socialists were appeased by the steady improvement in wages and their own growing strength in Parliament.

According to the Schumpeter school, this durable conservative coalition made Imperial Germany increasingly unstable. It isolated workers from a meaningful place in the social and political order and prevented the evolution to a better-integrated society. Failure to make timely constitutional reforms made the political system dangerously unresponsive.

Internationally, the effects are said to have been even worse. Agricultural protectionism embittered economic relations with Russia and thus fed the Russian entente with France. Industrial tariffs and dumping alienated Britain. Junker social and political hegemony, moreover, nurtured an antimodernist antipathy to industry which, in view of the Junker alliance with heavy industry, was conveniently deflected from its domestic object and projected outward into an intense ideological hostility toward Britain. Britain was believed to have all the vices of industry and Germany all the virtues of agriculture. Hence, it is said, an essentially spurious ideological position poisoned Anglo-German relations and made accommodation between the two industrial giants all the more unlikely. In short, Germany's diplomatic isolation was inherent in its domestic politics.

The Schumpeter View and the First World War

A Schumpeterian analysis obviously yields many insights about Imperial Germany, even if it seriously exaggerates the significance of Junker "hegemony." But as an explanation for the First World War, it presupposes a logical step linking domestic and international conflict that is not convincing. It is not enough merely to list all the cleavages, stresses, and irrationalities of the German political economy in order to show a convincing relationship between them and Germany's involvement in the war. It is not even enough to show how domestic cleavages led to frictions with foreign powers. That there can be a link between domestic and foreign conflict is, of course, obvious. Since Plato's time, the belief that a society not at peace with itself is unlikely to be at peace with its neighbors has been a commonplace of political philosophy. On the other hand, there are few moments in the life of modern nation-states when it has not been easy to find fundamental conflicts within their societies and political systems. Doubtless many of these inner tensions have been projected into external conflict. But international politics, like domestic, is nearly always full of active and potential conflicts. What makes these conflicts suddenly precipitate the massive violence of war? An analysis of the domestic sources of tension, if necessary to an understanding of international conflicts, is also insufficient.

It might be useful at this point to recall the last chapter's analysis of the causes of the First World War. Consciously or not, it was Britain, more than any other power, who turned the war into a general war. This is not to say that Britain caused the war, or was wrong to act as it did; it is only to say that Britain, whose weight on one side or the other was generally perceived to be decisive, chose not to play its traditional role of detached balancer and peacekeeper. By holding back as long as it did, Britain lost its deterrent effect on Germany, as well as the others; by coming in at the end, it denied Germany the possibility of winning a quick victory in a localized continental war. Why Britain behaved as it did is, of course, fertile if treacherous ground for further historical research and interpretation. Whatever such study may reveal, it will not show Anglo-German rivalry, misunderstanding, and mutual hatred irrelevant to Britain's decision. The causes for Anglo-German friction were obviously complex – cultural and geopolitical as well as economic. But surely economic competition had an obvious role. The Germans, with great skill and determination, were successfully penetrating British markets throughout the world. Moreover, the Germans were not only menacing Britain's world position, they were building a fleet expressly to challenge Britain's naval supremacy.

Of the many things about Imperial Germany that bothered the British, agricultural protectionism cannot have been very significant. Commercially, the British were not upset by Germany's grain tariffs but by the policy of industrial protectionism at home combined with aggressive dumping abroad. It was not the beleaguered Junker farmers who were the authors of that policy; nor were they, in fact, the promoters of the German fleet. In short, it was not the "obsolescent" Junker agrarians who dictated the policies that fed Anglo-German antagonism, but the forward-looking promoters of the new order – the industrialists and the middle-class National Liberals. These "modernist" groups, moreover, were hardly the passive observers of German policy that the Schumpeterian analysis implies. Although the continuing influence of the agrarians, both politically and culturally, was an obvious feature of Wilhelmine Germany, power was nevertheless clearly shifting to the new industrial classes. As the Caprivi episode suggests, the agrarian elite had lost the initiative.

Imperial Politics: A Broader View

If anything promoted Anglo-German antagonism, it was building a German battle fleet. Who was responsible? An intensive analysis of the forces that coalesced to pass the two Naval Laws, the first in 1898 and the second in 1900, can be found in Eckart Kehr's noted study, *Battleship Building and Party Politics in Germany, 1894-1901.* Kehr's analysis yields a number of general points relevant to the present discussion.

To begin with, pressure for the fleet certainly did not come from the Junkers. Neither farmers, who feared the taxes, nor the military, who feared a naval rival for funds and prestige, were at all favorable. Within the government, the prime mover was the kaiser himself, who believed a fleet essential to Germany's future as a "world" power. Inextricably tied to the kaiser's notion of Germany as a world power, competing with Britain, was acceptance of

Germany's transformation from an agricultural into a modern industrial nation. The kaiser's view was commonplace. From the start, building a fleet was seen as part of a world imperialist policy, justified by the imperatives of economic expansion. The navy, in short, had a good Leninist view: War and industrialization were seen as inextricably linked. The Junker army, by contrast, continued to see war as a knightly struggle of power elites, with little if any reference to economic motives. The enemies, moreover, were not Britain, but Russia and France.

The principal minister to shape and affect the kaiser's naval ambitions was Admiral von Tirpitz, who was not a Junker but a politically gifted technocrat of middle-class origins. Tirpitz not only formulated and administered a coherent plan for ambitious naval development, but organized a vast public relations campaign through the press, universities, and the middle-class media generally. Outside the government, the navy's most powerful backing came from big industry, Krupp in particular. Industrial patronage supported a gigantic mass pressure group, the German Navy League.

Industry was overwhelmingly favorable to the fleet — interested both in the profits to be made from its construction and servicing and sanguine about its usefulness for imperial purposes. Krupp, whose growth depended heavily on government contracts, had direct profit motives, as did other steel, shipbuilding, mining, and chemical interests. But naval enthusiasm was by no means limited to the heavy industries. The newer industries, like Emil Rathenau's AEG, although they disapproved of the protectionist tariffs promoted by heavy industry, nevertheless were also enthusiastic supporters of the fleet. Also among the strong supporters were German commercial firms, centered in old Hansa cities. In the business world, only financial interests appear to have been tepid, even if their enthusiasm grew with the bond issues used to finance naval armament.

In short, of all the major organized national interest groups, aside from labor, only the agrarians were opposed to the fleet. Yet in the end they came to support it. Kehr's explanation shows their predicament and weakness. Junker agriculture turned to party and interest-group politics to protect itself against cheap grain imports from Russia and the United States. To survive, the beleaguered Junker farmers wanted a policy of agricultural autarchy, a policy that meant conflict with Russia. This political mobilization of agriculture was precipitated by Caprivi's free-trade policy, the means by which he hoped to develop adequate markets for Germany's industry. Like a good Prussian liberal, Caprivi apparently believed free trade would lead to international harmony. And like a good Prussian general, he was preoccupied with the threat of an imminent war on two fronts. He therefore worked for an Anglo-German alliance. Germany would not need a great fleet, Caprivi hoped. Britain would protect Germany's vital imports.

Whatever its merits, Caprivi's free-trade strategy was anathema to the agrarians. Logically, the Junker policy, which would make an enemy of Russia, called for an alliance with Britain. From class interest, Kehr argues, the agrarians ought to have promoted an Anglo-Junker alliance against German industry. For the real rivals to Junker predominance in Germany were the industrialists. Junker hegemony could have been maintained only by stifling Germany's industrial development. Such a policy was impossible not only because of the opposition it would have aroused from industry, but because it suffered from a fatal internal contradiction, even from a Junker perspective. A protectionist Germany that remained agricultural could never expect to sustain a modern army to counter France and Russia. Had the Junker agrarians tried to impose such an antiindustrial policy, they would have defined their fundamental class interests in a fashion to put themselves in opposition not only to the clear interests of the nation in general terms, but also to the interest of the Prussian army – their own creation and justification. To avoid so exposed and contradictory a position, the Junker gentry were driven to compromise with the rising bourgeoisie. That compromise emerged in Bismarck's protectionist coalition and Miquel's *Sammlungspolitik*. As Kehr puts it:

In order to procure the grain import duties, which signified economic-political opposition to Russia, they were ready to support industry's competitive struggle with England. The profound dualism of German foreign policy in 1914, implying both England and Russia as enemies, has its internal foundation in Miquel's policy of compromise between industry and agriculture. From the standpoint of internal politics, this compromise of interests of the warring classes rested upon the Agrarians' approving a navy for industry, with industry approving the tariffs for the Agrarians, and both together keeping the proletariat from gaining control of state power. The foreign policy correlative of the *Sammlungspolitik* was the implementation of agriculture's anti-Russian policy while giving up its friendship with England, and the carrying through of the competitive struggle of industry and trade with England by finally relinquishing Russia and allowing it to become the object of exploitation by French capital and by definitely abandoning the execution of liberal tendencies at home.[3]

For the agrarians, the solution was far from ideal. Although it protected their farms, it also fostered industry's preeminence. But the Junkers had no alternative. As Kehr sees it:

The Conservatives did not approve the fleet because they loved it but because they feared it, not because they agreed with its tendencies but because in case of their opposition to it they must fear an aggravation of those same tendencies. That inclination of aristocrats of which Ranke once spoke, to assist in the exercise of despotism only in order not to experience despotism themselves – this negative motive for internal conservative power politics found its foreign-policy parallel in the hesitant and painfully cautious entry of the conservatives into imperialism.[4]

---

[3] Eckart Kehr, *Battleship Building and Party Politics in Germany 1894–1901* (1930) (Chicago: University of Chicago Press, 1973), pp. 275–6.

[4] Ibid., p. 345.

If they did not go along, they feared a new alliance that would leave them out.

Kehr's detailed analysis of the parliamentary politics of fleet building gives a highly sophisticated and credible view of the imperial political system. That system emerges as plural and shifting, as might be expected from so diverse and rapidly evolving a society. The Junkers were not an all-dominant class but a besieged and overextended interest group, without the initiative but with a qualified power of veto, particularly as long as the Prussian franchise was unreformed. With the institutional remnants of their old hegemony, they sought concessions to mitigate their decline. Giant industry was emerging as the dominant force in German society. Even if underrepresented in quantity and quality within the Parliament, industry was nevertheless in a position to press its needs effectively upon the state. The kaiser himself, and the technocratic elites of the civil administration, were highly sensitive to industry's needs and demands. The navy, as Kehr shows, was self-consciously tied to a vision of itself as the necessary imperial arm of national industrial development and commerce. It was this imperialist industrial consciousness that saw Britain as Germany's principal enemy. By contrast, the Junker agrarians, and indeed the military, saw Russia and France as their principal enemies and Britain as their traditional ally. Left to their own devices, Kehr argues, the Junkers would have protected their agriculture and throttled domestic industrialization.

What remains, then, of the Schumpeterian thesis? If the Junkers were not the architects of the anti-British world policy, they did, it can be argued, play a major role in determining the shape of that world policy. For a start, the agrarians may be said at least to have held the balance among the competing types of industry. Thanks to the agrarians, government policy tilted toward the industrial tariffs demanded by heavy industry rather than the liberal policies advocated by the newer and lighter industries – like AEG and Siemens represented in Parliament by the Progressive Union. But whereas a more liberal external and perhaps internal coalition might have made an accommodation with the Social Democrats easier, still Siemens and Rathenau were no less imperialistic than Krupp or antagonistic to Britain. All supported the fleet. Indeed, the two giant electrical companies were Clapham's models for the mercantilist and aggressive international firm typical of German industry and world commerce. In short, even if the agrarians favored one type of industry over another, they were hardly responsible for Germany's outward world thrust, and hence its rivalry with Britain.

The agrarians were decisive, of course, in fostering antagonism with Russia. Without the agricultural tariffs, an industrial Germany and an agricultural Russia might conceivably have made a natural alliance. But as the Russians themselves began to industrialize on a large scale in the early twentieth century, any such relationship was unlikely to persist.

In conclusion, it is hard to escape from the rather traditional Leninist view that Imperial Germany's international problem sprang less from its "feudal" remnants than from the timing of its capitalist development. The Germans' problem lay in their late-blooming vigor. In their era of rapid growth, the Imperial Germans were not all that different from the other Western countries – in particular, Britain and the United States. To be sure, Prussia doted on its Junker army, but was liberal Britannia any less solicitous of its fleet? Or was that too acquired in a fit of absent-mindedness? And what of the huge British military establishment run out of India? But if the Germans were no more aggressive, they were certainly less fortunate. Unlike the British, they did not find the world empty before them, and, unlike the Americans, they lacked a vast continental backyard of their own. Boxed in as they were, their rise was too swift for the international system to accommodate without a major war. But it is difficult to lay the responsibility for that war solely on the Germans, and even more difficult to ascribe it to the special economic and political interests of their agriculturalists.

There is, of course, a more subtle version of the Schumpeter argument. Germany's problem, it is said, sprang not so much from the predominance of Junker interests as of Junker values. Hence the arrogant, power-hungry materialism characteristic of Imperial Germany. To be sure, the Prussian officer was a powerful ideal, a model for the German gentleman. But what was that ideal? In fairness to traditional Germany, the model was less the swaggering bully of grade B movies than the brave, dutiful, disciplined, gentle Christian knight of the medieval tradition – the Joachim Ziemssen of *The Magic Mountain*. Can the German preoccupation with power really be laid to that tradition? – a large and elusive subject, taken up again in Chapter 6.

5

Hitler and the German Problem

How German was Hitler?

Nowhere in German history is the question of continuity more significant or difficult than with the Nazi regime. Some, to be sure, find Hitler a unique and terrible aberration – the expression not of the course of German history, but of exceptional circumstances and malignant genius. Many others, however, see in Hitler the quintessential manifestation of the German problem. Certainly no regime could demonstrate more clearly aggression abroad and totalitarianism at home.

Like most historical phenomena, Hitler's regime did have many elements of continuity with the past. The links seem particularly clear in foreign policy. In his general geopolitical analysis, Hitler was similar in many respects not only to annexationists like Ludendorff, but also to Beth-mann-Hollweg and Rathenau. All were concerned with what they saw as Germany's precarious position in the coming world of superstates. Hitler's writings and conversations reveal his continual reflecting on Germany's historic predicament and the various solutions to it. In *Mein Kampf,* as well as in later writings, Hitler analyzed with exceptional acuteness the traditional Great German and Little German options – their advantages, costs, and preconditions. These geopolitical ideas stayed with him throughout the twistings and turnings of a meteoric career, and had changed remarkably little when he dictated his *Testament* in 1945. His historic mission, as he saw it, was to resolve that German geopolitical problem, regardless of the cost to other nations or to his own generation of Germans.

Whatever the other similarities, Hitler did separate himself clearly from his imperial predecessors in assigning a vital geopolitical significance to race. Hitler's racial policy was not only anti-Semitism, but a systematic plan to exterminate and replace the population of large contiguous areas to the east. Germanic types were to populate a Germany stretching from the Low Countries to the Urals. Others had believed a large German imperial sphere in Europe to be a geopolitical necessity. But no one in power had seriously set out to extend national Germany by clearing out and repopulating the entire Eastern region of Europe. Obviously, these racial views greatly affected Hitler's analysis of the German Problem, his options for resolving it, and their acceptability in the world at large.

It is tempting, if historically unjustified, to abstract Hitler's racial policy from his geopolitical analysis. As a geopolitician, it could be said, Hitler was a German. As a racist, he was an Austrian, with the peculiar preoccupations of the Dual Monarchy's petit-bourgeois German minority. From such a distinction, a number of intriguing speculations easily follow: Had Hitler been more German and less Austrian, race would not have mattered. Hence, it might be implied: The Germans were not really to blame for the bestiality of Hitler's racism. And more subtly: Without the preoccupation with race, German hegemony might have been sustained in Europe. Hence the Germans were not even responsible for Hitler's failure. We can return to these speculations after examining Hitler's view and policies in greater detail.

Fundamental Geopolitical Ideas

Hitler's analysis of the German Problem was related to a highly conscious philosophical world view. His political philosophy reflected the Darwinism common to most geopolitical writers. History was the struggle of peoples, a struggle almost inevitably competitive. To exist and flourish, a people needed enough territory to support themselves properly. Hence the task of foreign policy was to occupy and hold adequate living space. To succeed, a people needed to organize themselves within a state able to mobilize and direct the collective strength. A people's strength was drawn from a combination of "personality value" – the capacity of its leadership, and "race value" – the genetic endowment of its masses. Hitler's racial ideas were woven into his general political philosophy. "Mixing," he believed, usually depreciated a people's race value. Multinational states that were imperial in scope and cosmopolitan in their elites, like his native Austria-Hungary, were therefore anathema to him. States should remain national, he insisted. And nationality was essentially genetic and hence not easily extended. His other component of strength, "personality value" required a political system that developed and gave power to men of exceptional talent, unlike parliamentary democracy, which shrank from exceptional leaders and fragmented a people into quarreling interest groups. In short, to conduct a successful foreign policy and thus flourish in history, a people needed unity within an authoritarian national state.

Hitler saw the Germans, despite their exceptional race value, failing in history. The failure was both international and domestic. Thanks to an inadequate political system,

Germany had not succeeded in gaining vital living space for a rapidly rising population. Time was running out. To reverse the decline became Hitler's desperate mission.

Hitler saw five options for dealing with Germany's lack of living space. The first two meant limiting the population – either through birth control or emigration. Both possibilities were harmful, he believed, as they inexorably reduced the population's race value. Birth control meant fewer children more carefully nurtured, whereas genetic health demanded a greater number more ruthlessly selected. Emigration, he argued, sent away the bravest and most venturesome and enriched others with the flower of the German race.

A third option lay in "internal colonization" – a more intensive and scientific cultivation of existing land. Such practices should certainly be encouraged, he believed, but their effects would be too limited to resolve the fundamental problem. Meanwhile, excessive expectations from technology risked undermining the national will to confront sterner but more promising alternatives.

Hitler's fourth option called for turning a territorially restricted national state into an export machine. This was, in effect, Hitler's definition of a Little German or world policy. Surplus goods would be traded for the food that could not be raised at home. The British had chosen this path in the early nineteenth century, Hitler noted, and Imperial or "bourgeois nationalist" Germany had unwisely chosen to imitate them. Hitler professed to dislike mushrooming industrial growth and urbanization, particularly when not counterbalanced by an agricultural population and production adequate for self-sufficiency. Such a situation was not only unhealthy for racial vitality, he argued, but dangerous to national security. For without Britain's ability to control and defend an adequate system of markets and raw materials, a nation was left in precarious dependence upon the goodwill of others. Moreover, too many countries were expecting to live off their export surpluses. An intensifying conflict for markets and supplies was therefore inevitable. And it was naive, Hitler argued, to expect such commercial conflicts to remain peaceful. Once foreign competition threatened a nation's well-being, it would use military force to alter the commercial game. The First World War had shown how ill-favored Germany was to challenge Britain as a world commercial power. Moreover, no European country could, in the end, expect its exports to compete with those of American industry, which drew strength from a vast home market.

Hitler's arguments led inexorably to his fifth option: territorial expansion – not in remote parts of the world, but in lands contiguous to Germany. The German people were not to be scattered around the globe, but kept together with adequate space to grow. They were to find that space by conquering neighboring peoples and settling in their territories. Germans and others of Germanic stock, properly reconditioned, were to colonize the spaces gradually cleared of Slavs and other supposedly inferior breeds.

Pursuing either world or continental options, Hitler believed, meant war. His continental option obviously required a war with Russia. And the world option, Hitler believed, meant war sooner or later with Britain and the United States.

Imperial German Failings

Hitler was highly critical of his post-Bismarckian predecessors. He saw the imperial era as a sorry record of drift and vacillation. After Bismarck's great achievement, no one had dealt with the vital foreign policy problem of the new Reich. Imperial policy had toyed with ideas of territorial expansion to the east, but had shrunk from decisive action. Instead, the Second Reich's dominant "national bourgeoisie" made Germany a giant export machine, and dreamed fatuously of "peaceful conquest" through industrial and commercial expansion. Such a policy made sharp rivalry with Britain inevitable, a competition which could remain peaceful only insofar as Germany did not seriously threaten Britain's position. Because Britain's great commercial system had been built by force, Britain could be expected to defend it by force. Hence, Hitler concluded, when Imperial Germany began halfheartedly to build a navy, Britain predictably responded with an alarm that soon turned to energetic hatred.

In Hitler's view, Germany's export orientation and consequent challenge to Britain was a mistaken policy. But had a national-bourgeois Germany wished to pursue it, he argued, elementary prudence required coming to terms with Russia. Instead, a sentimental alliance with Austria-Hungary made Germany the principal enemy of the Russians and of all those other Slavs who eagerly awaited the Habsburg demise. As Hitler saw it, the Austrian alliance brought Germany more enemies than support, even within a purely Eastern European context. But with an English war in the offing, the Habsburg tie was madness. Germany should have destroyed Austria, absorbed its Germans, and become the patron of its liberated Slavs. And, in any event, Hitler decided, an Imperial Germany bent on rivalry with Britain should have gone to war earlier, rather than allowing Britain to organize Germany's encirclement at leisure. As it was, a feckless German government, hoping for peaceful economic conquest, followed contradictory policies that joined Russia and Britain against it. In the end, an ocean of German blood was sacrificed for the confused pursuit of contradictory aims.

Hitler's view of imperial foreign policy makes it seem a Germanic variant of British muddling through. The Imperial Reich ruined itself, he believed, because its leaders, who naively assumed that economic conflict could be peaceful, could not choose decisively between worldwide and continental strategies. Why, Hitler asked himself, should the German people have been so badly led? The bourgeois nationalist empire, he decided, had long been in decay. Parliamentary democracy gradually undermined aristocratic and monarchical authority, while persisting monarchical forms inhibited a conservative reaction. And just as political liberalism had undermined the governing class, economic liberalism had disrupted the national economic and social system. An internationally oriented capitalism, dominated by finance capital and the stock exchange, had depersonalized ownership and dehumanized labor. The laborer was sweated, alienated from his work, and crowded into pestilential cities. An irresponsible bourgeoisie proved indifferent either to the suffering of the new proletariat or to the disintegration of the community. Heartless international capitalism spawned its proletarian counterpart, international Marxist socialism. As the bourgeois capitalists exploited proletarian labor, the Social Democratic politicians exploited proletarian outrage. The worker, abandoned by a bourgeoisie too selfish to lead, learned class war and hatred of all authority. As a result, the country grew bitterly divided and increasingly ungovernable – a condition amply illustrated, Hitler argued, by the imperial regime's prewar incompetence and wartime collapse.

Race

Left thus, Hitler's domestic critique of Imperial Germany would constitute an attack on classic liberalism such as might easily have been found in many nationalist conservative or indeed socialist writers, not only in Germany but in most other capitalist countries. Hitler, however, linked his nationalist antiliberalism with anti-Semitism, a politically potent if logically unnecessary combination. Germans grew alienated from their society, he argued, because that society was increasingly directed by aliens within it, the Jews. Jews for Hitler were not simply a metaphor for the evils of modern industrialism, but a real political force — indeed a nation, even if nonterritorial. Hitler admitted, at the end of his life at least, that the Jewish race was more a political label than a genetic reality. But, he argued, a modern Jewish community, nurtured by centuries of persecution, did exist and form a separate people, incorrigibly unassimilable into other nations. Even if every modern Jew probably had at least a little original Jewish blood, greatly mixed to be sure, the real bond among the Jewish people was "the characteristic mental make-up of [the Jew's] race which renders him impervious to the processes of assimilation . . . — proof of the superiority of the mind over the flesh."[1] According to Hitler, the Jew, belonging to his own nation, lived as a parasite inside the national societies of others. He flourished by disintegrating other nations from within. Under Jewish inspiration, the host nation was poisoned from both sides of the political spectrum. On the Right, the Jews were the masters and propagators of that international finance capitalism that depersonalized ownership and work. On the Left, Jews were the inventors and propagators of Marxism, which exploited worker discontent to create class war. Thus, the seemingly opposite Jewish forces combined to disintegrate the national unity of their hosts.

Hitler used the Bolshevik revolution as his primary example. Marxism and finance capitalism, he argued, had combined to destroy the czarist state. Bolshevism, led by Jewish intellectuals and agitators, was merely the prelude to Jewish financial domination. Hitler eventually came to argue that Stalin, by defeating Trotsky and resurrecting Russian nationalism, had robbed the Jews of their victory. In any event, as the Jews had behaved in Russia, Hitler

[1] Adolf Hitler, *The Testament of Adolf Hitler*, edited by François Genoud (London: Cassel, 1961), p. 54.

argued, so they behaved in every state whose internal weakness presented them with an opportunity. It had been Russia's turn in 1917 and Germany's in 1918. As a nation ripe for disintegration, Weimar Germany had been increasingly dominated by Jewish power using money, the press, leftist parties and trade unions, and, if necessary, terror. Alien capital had relentlessly penetrated Weimar's economy, and class conflict had intensified. Weimar democracy had prevented any strong government that might have brought the aliens under national control. Meanwhile, Weimar's foreign policy aimed at placating France — for Hitler a sure sign of German debility.

Hitler's Program

At this dark hour in German history, Hitler wrote in *Mein Kampf,* National Socialism had sprung forth to rally the vitality of the German people. The Nazis had risen to put a stop to Germany's domestic decline and reassert its interests in the world at large.

Hitler spelled out his domestic program in various writings and interviews before he came to power. The Nazis would give the German people an authoritarian national state, he promised. Fascist corporatism would end the economic and political exploitation of labor and contain capitalism within clearly defined national goals and social norms. Social Democracy and Marxism would be crushed; foreign capital and alien finance expelled. The economy would disengage from the thrashings of an irrational world system and move toward autarchic independence.

Once National Socialism had rejuvenated the domestic base, Hitler promised, Germany would once again conduct a serious foreign policy. Its aim, Hitler stated again and again, would never be merely to restore the old borders. Restoration was a policy that was tactically stupid, because it reinforced the bonds among the Allies, and strategically irrelevant, because it left unresolved Germany's basic problem of living space. If the German people were to be a great force in the next century, Hitler argued, Germany would have to break out of its territorial straitjacket and seize new lands. Otherwise, in the coming world of giants, Germany's fate was to be dominated by those countries whose foreign policies had not failed.

Not only Hitler's goals, but also his fundamental strategy, were laid out clearly enough in his early writings, and varied remarkably little in the years that followed. France and Russia were, he believed, Germany's two permanent strategic enemies. France's own grand design a – "negrified" empire from the Rhine to the Congo – required a harmless Germany, shorn of the left bank of the Rhine and broken into fragments. Germany would have to defeat France and squelch its pretensions forever. And because Russia was both the instrument of Bolshevism and the source for Germany's *Lebensraum,* a decisive struggle with Russia was also inevitable.

Hitler's grand design could never be achieved, he realized, without allies. Both Italy and Britain, he believed, could be won over. As an unsatisfied nationalist power with Mediterranean and Balkan ambitions, Italy was France's natural enemy and therefore would naturally ally with Germany. And if the ground were prepared properly, Hitler convinced himself, Britain would come to accept Germany's continental ambitions. Britain would not oppose German continental hegemony as long as it were not used as the springboard for world power. Thus, according to Hitler, Britain had not opposed Napoleon for his European conquests, but for his extra-European adventures. France, not Germany, was Britain's natural enemy in Europe; for the French combined European with world ambitions. A Germany that clearly renounced world economic and political ambitions, and instead built an autarchic European superstate, had no reason to arouse British enmity – particularly as German goals were to be fulfilled at the expense not only of imperialist France, but also of Bolshevik Russia.

Hitler expected Britain's friendship for an additional reason. The island empire, he believed, was increasingly threatened by the inexorable rise of American economic and naval power. Britain needed a friendly continental colossus as a counterpoise to the American giant. Otherwise, Britain's imperial system would be at the mercy of an economic and military power it could not hope to resist. The United States, still isolationist and preoccupied, was not yet ready for world power. But time was running out for both Britain and Germany.

Would the British see their own interest or be bemused by their American ties? For Hitler, the principal danger lay in the power of the Jews in both Anglo-Saxon countries. The fundamental Jewish interests, according to Hitler, were anti-Nazi and pro-Bolshevik. With their traditional power in Britain, and their growing influence in the United States, especially over Roosevelt, Jews had become powerful partisans of the Anglo-American "special relation." The British Jews, Hitler argued, had tipped their hand as early as 1922, when they reinforced the strong American pressure against renewing the Anglo-Japanese alliance. But this Anglo-American special relation, although in the interest of international Jewry, was not in the interest of the British Empire, Hitler argued. Thus, a national British policy, rather than one dictated by alien forces and interests, would naturally gravitate Britain toward alliance with a resurgent Germany. Otherwise the two countries would ruin each other – to the profit of the Americans and the Bolsheviks.

Hitler and the Second World War: Appeasement

Did Hitler deliberately plan and launch the war in 1939, or did he blunder into it? Were his aims such that he might have been appeased without a war? Even today these questions are difficult to deal with. For not only is the historical evidence still indecisive, but the issues remain highly charged with politics. Much of postwar American imperial ideology, for example, has been based upon two theories, both elevated to the status of political myths: Churchill's myth that blames the war on Allied appeasement and Cordell Hull's myth that blames the war on Axis autarchy. Neither theory, of course, is self-evidently valid.

Disagreement over appeasement goes back to the thirties and continues in subtle ways to reflect divisions among Britain's political elites. Newly released papers and diaries rekindle the old arguments. As with the First World War, the question of war aims and responsibilities has several dimensions. Three seem particularly relevant. First, what were the geopolitical perspectives that framed Hitler's statesmanship? Second, how did the war actually start? Finally, what domestic compulsions shaped Hitler's policy?

The first question has absorbed our attention so far. According to Hitler the geopolitician, a war with Russia and France was inevitable. At the same time, Hitler's geopolitical strategy called for a deal with Britain. Germany would gain hegemony over the Continent and Britain would be confirmed in its empire. Had Britain been willing to appease Germany to this extent, Hitler seems to have believed that Britain and Germany need not have gone to war.

On the second question, how the war started, there is sharp disagreement, but recent scholarship suggests certain broad conclusions relevant to our general study. A. J. P. Taylor's celebrated *Origins of the Second World War* sparked the postwar debate among the British and Americans. Taylor argued that Hitler's prewar diplomacy was not determined by the grand plans of *Mein Kampf*, at least not in some straightforward mechanical fashion. Instead, Taylor saw Hitler as an opportunistic politician, exploiting the sympathies and weaknesses of the Allies in order to restore Germany's prewar position and bolster his shaky regime. Taylor makes his points with customary brilliance. He notes Hitler's tactical opportunism and lack of serious preparation for general war. Nevertheless, the argument is ambiguous to some extent. Hitler most certainly did not limit his ambitions to regaining the pre-1914 borders, a policy that he attacked scathingly when advocated by others. Whatever the vagueness of his timetable, Hitler wanted hegemony over Europe, and *Lebensraum* in the east, and had no intention of trading these goals for minor territorial concessions. But Taylor has got hold of a fundamental point, even if he overstates it. Hitler did seem genuinely surprised, in a sense even trapped, by Britain's sudden firmness over Poland. Hitler's claim on Danzig were unexceptionable, at least according to those principles of self-determination upon which the Versailles settlement was presumably based. Under the circumstances, the appropriate question seems less why Hitler was surprised than why the Danzig question provoked the British into abandoning appeasement and guaranteeing Poland.

Some recent studies of Cabinet documents appear to confirm and elaborate an old theory. The guarantee to Poland was not so much a reversal of British policy as its logical conclusion. Chamberlain, for all his dislike of Bolshevism, was not finally willing to make the deal needed to appease Hitler. In other words, he was not willing to concede Germany hegemony over Eastern Europe. What was called appeasement, the abandoning of Czechoslovakia, was a conditional concession, justified by the need to buy time for British rearmament.

A recent book by Simon Newman, *March 1939:The British Guarantee to Poland,* charts the debate through the official documents. His conclusion, in brief:

... Britain never intended Germany to have a free hand in eastern Europe at all. Thus the guarantee to Poland should not be interpreted as a revolution in British foreign policy ... but should be seen as the culmination, or rather the explicit manifestation, of a strand of British policy going back to before September 1938 which has until recently been overlooked or ignored – the attempt to stem German expansionism in eastern Europe by any means short of war but in the last resort by war itself.[2]

Chamberlain was acutely conscious of the delicacy of Britain's situation. Britain could not hope to defeat simultaneously Germany and Italy in Europe and Japan in Asia. Neither the United States nor Russia could be relied upon as Allies and, in any event, calling upon them would in itself profoundly upset the world balance. Britain would therefore try to reach agreement with some of its potential enemies, but not at any price. Germany would be offered limited commercial concessions in the British Empire and perhaps colonies outside Europe. But it would be opposed in Europe by Britain's economic power and, if absolutely necessary, by force. The government's policy gradually grew more militant after the Munich Conference. By November 1938, the British had commenced a campaign of economic warfare as part of a more general policy of heightened resistance to German predominance in the Balkans. Throughout the preceding period an Inter-Departmental Committee under Sir Frederick Leith-Ross had been meeting to formulate a fundamental policy. Interestingly enough, the committee's stated rationale for opposing Germany was explicitly economic – a principled resistance to autarchy. Halifax, the foreign minister, endorsed the report and added his own memorandum, which deserves quotation at length. Arguments for giving Germany a free hand assumed, Halifax wrote:

that the trade between Germany and the South-Eastern European countries will be of an orthodox, liberal or free trade character based on the free exchange of goods and payment by free exchange. But this has not been the case in the past and is unlikely to be the case in the future, unless, as is just possible, there is a fundamental change in Ger-

[2] Simon Newman, *March 1939: The British Guarantee to Poland* (Oxford: Clarendon Press, 1976). pp. 5–6.

many's economic and financial policy. It seems, at present, far more likely that any economic dominance that Germany may attain in these countries will result in their economic vassalage to Germany and to German economic doctrine, and that German foreign exchange restrictions and autarchic aims will become factors conditioning and moulding the economic life of each of them. This, in fact, seems certain so long as Germany refuses to envisage the depreciation of the mark and to relax her exchange controls, and so long as she insists that these countries shall receive payment for their exports in German goods, wanted or unwanted. Moreover, the short-term credits by London to Germany, both before and since the war, have been frozen and have proved a source of great embarrassment and, indeed, of danger to the international credit of London. We could not afford to lock up further resources in Germany, so long as she maintains system of exchange control; nor to advance funds to the Danubian countries so long as their trade with Germany only produces blocked marks. While, therefore, Germany, for one reason or another, is unwilling to lift her exchange controls, the arguments in favor of permitting her a free hand in these countries would seem largely to fall to the ground.[3]

Because the entire region accounted for around 1 percent of total British trade, the overriding political significance of Britain's opposition seems clear. The British were unwilling to concede Germany even the limited sphere that Hitler had already largely achieved, let alone the greater Germany of his dreams. In the Second War War, as in the First World War, Britain had no intention of acquiescing in continental hegemony to the Germans. Under the circumstances, a general war was no doubt inevitable. That it broke out over Poland was, in a sense, more a British than a German initiative. As it happened, whereas British military planners discounted Czech defense, they believed the Poles to have a formidable army. Without the Polish army in the Allied camp, they saw the military balance shifting to the Germans. Rather than risk the loss, Britain rushed in with a guarantee to bolster Polish resolve. Thus, Britain's tactical appeasement came to an abrupt end. Whatever the

[3] Ibid., pp. 47–8.

military wisdom of conceding Hitler Czechoslovakia while denying him Poland, the basic British strategy seems clear: They never intended to appease Germany in Europe on the scale needed to avoid a war. Hitler, it should be said, had few illusions about Chamberlain's policy at the end, even if he was caught off balance by the Polish guarantee. Certainly Hitler's appetite for *Lebensraum*, as we know, hardly sprang from his perception that Britain was "sleeping." Hitler, in fact, profoundly distrusted Chamberlain and believed himself to have been outmaneuvered even at Munich. Chamberlain's concessions prevented an earlier war that Hitler thought would have favored Germany. In short, the Second World War came not from misunderstandings, but because Germany and Britain were, once more, set on a collision course over Europe.

Other recent accounts argue that Chamberlain, himself, wanted to appease Hitler, or perhaps to pit Germany against Russia, but that the combination of Hitler's determination to defeat France, plus the powerful antipathy against Germany in the Cabinet, the Parliament, and the British public made such a policy impossible. It will doubtless be a long time before such issues are settled. In any event, whatever the view of Chamberlain's intentions, the consequences for Germany were the same: Britain would not acquiesce in German hegemony over Europe. That a Prime Minister might have wanted to appease, and failed, only confirms the inevitability of the Anglo-German conflict.

Hitler and the Second World War: Autarchy

Was Hitler driven to war by his illiberal economy? Here the analyst is confronted by the ghost of Cordell Hull. If the First World War illustrates the difficulties of fitting an "outward looking" Germany into the world's political-economic system, the Second is supposed to show the equally grievous consequences of German autarchy. Newman's study exposes the aversion that Hitler's miniature continental system aroused in British circles before the war. The American State Department was even more hostile. As Roosevelt's secretary of state never ceased preaching, trading blocs led to war. The dictum was applied to Japan, where American policy made it almost a self-fulfilling prophecy. It was meant to apply no less to Germany. Hull's *Memoirs* leave the impression that Hitler's major crimes were not racism and mass murder but tariffs and exchange controls. That Hitler's autarchy was a crime, intimately connected with his domestic tyranny and foreign aggression, is a view that persists to the present day. But what was Hitler's prewar "autarchy"? How well did it work? Did it create domestic pressure that compelled a war of conquest? And what, indeed, does the history of the Nazi regime tell in general about the economic viability of Germany's continental option?

It is difficult to assess how the autarchic economic model might have worked in "normal" circumstances – if, indeed, "normal" can ever be applied to the Nazi regime. Hitler's entire reign was a long succession of exceptional situations – depression, rearmament, and war itself. The record of the 1930s is nevertheless suggestive. As the economist John Kenneth Galbraith has noted, prewar Nazi economic policy represents a rather singular illustration of Keynesian practices thoroughly and successfully applied. To end unemployment, Hitler carried out a vast program of labor-intensive public works and residential construction. At the same time, he began to reorganize agriculture. In due course, an ambitious program to achieve self-sufficiency stimulated industry; new capacity was built up in certain fields and synthetic substitutes were developed on a grand scale. In 1936 came rearmament.

Hitler successfully financed the recovery through a combination of his own willfulness and the fertile imagination of his "wizard" Schacht. Trade and exchange controls, standstills, and a final moratorium on foreign debts insulated Hitler's Germany from these international capital flows that had so disrupted Weimar. As the economy gradually reached full employment, however, and as Hitler insisted on rearming without reducing civilian consumption, inflationary shortages and balance-of-payments difficulties grew increasingly serious. Hitler was undeterred. Economists, he argued, needlessly complicated their subject. Elaborate theories tied inflation to the growth of the money supply. But inflation, after all, came only when sellers put up prices. Controlling inflation, like everything else, was finally a matter of power and will. Whatever the expansion of credit, a resolute government, armed with concentration camps, could always control inflation. Ostentatiously jailing a few profiteers would keep the others in line. Hitler's solution, which did indeed suppress inflation remarkably well, was more regimentation for agriculture, labor, and industry. The style of regimentation varied in each sphere. Labor was most strictly controlled, but given security, an honored place in the regime's ideology, and extensive programs of free recreation. Agriculture was given security and profits, but farmers were told what to plant and could not sell land freely. Industrialists were left in possession of their firms, but increasingly had to operate them within an apparatus of state allocation and pricing. Most continued to profit, and some, like I. G. Farben, did very well. In general, the planning apparatus was loose, not to say chaotic, in many respects – not least because Hitler, like Roosevelt, let opposing forces in his government struggle inconclusively for as long as possible.

For all his brutal willfulness, Hitler remained, it seems, highly solicitous of domestic morale and support for the regime. His policy before the war was delicately balanced between securing his domestic base and preparing his historic mission. Thus, while he did rearm, he greatly exaggerated the extent of rearmament to his contemporaries and was careful not to curtail civilian consumption. As a result, Germany was surprisingly unready for a long war. Indeed, not until 1943 was the economy really fully mobilized. Hitler, not unlike Bethmann, apparently gambled on blitzkrieg. If he won a quick war, Germany would enter a new era of solidly based prosperity; short-range problems of suppressed inflation would seem trivial in comparison with the vast acquisitions of territory and resources. And if he could not win a quick war, and the Anglo-Saxons mobilized fully against him, all was probably lost in any event.

Hitler's measured progress toward rearmament should not be read as a lack of zeal for his continental ambitions. He was, of course, highly pragmatic about means and always prepared to drop ideology when it suited him. He attracted and used all sorts of ideologues — socialists, agrarians, corporatists, and racists. He also made great use of the technocrats – especially as he needed them to prepare for war. But Hitler was not merely a cynical manipulator of ideas, without any convictions of his own. It is true that he soon dropped the more visionary National Socialist schemes provided, for example, by Feder or the Strassers. Some of these ideas doubtless proved silly as well as inconvenient, particularly as Hitler was struggling to consolidate his new regime. Others, like the resettlement of Germans on eastern land – the prerequisite for his new autarchic Germany, obviously had to be put off until the war was won. But the horrendous racial program against both Jews and Slavs, carried out at great economic, political, and military cost during the war itself, seems ample testimony to the seriousness of Hitler's ultimate goals. Hitler was, alas, a man with the courage of his convictions.

Many German conservatives, like Rauschning and Schacht, fervently wished otherwise. They looked to a new order to avoid the uncertainty and waste of liberal capital-ism while stabilizing society in more traditional values. They were content with the regime's early economic and diplomatic successes and hoped a domesticated Hitler would abandon his grander projects. Many grew disillusioned as Hitler revealed himself to be not some populist, authoritarian Keynesian, but a "voice of destruction." But Hitler's "madness" was inherent in his geopolitical analysis. No stable resolution of Germany's problems could be reached, he believed, until Germany had the control of Europe. Only a successful war with Russia could give the German economy a sound foundation for the future. Without that territorial foundation any success would be transitory – an interlude before the old coalition organized itself once more to crush the German upstart.

Well before the war, as the previous section notes, Hitler was reaching out toward that eastern economic space that he coveted. A tributary economic zone, gradually created in Eastern and Southeastern Europe, became a significant adjunct to the Nazi regime's prewar autarchic economy. Because Germany was the principal market for these countries, and liberal trade had collapsed, Germany's neighbors were more than willing to enter its economic orbit. An inconvertible, overvalued mark, useful only for German goods, tied the Balkan economies to a German currency zone, a restoration, in effect, of that prewar Central European system that had so impressed Keynes in his *Economic Consequences of the Peace*. As a pattern for an eventual continental autarchy, such a relationship might not have been so unattractive, particularly in contrast to the unstable liberal system of the interwar era. But Hitler's racial ideas made any such long-range relationship highly unpromising for the Slavs.

Similarly, even the larger' continental bloc Hitler established after 1940 suggested many economic advantages for all Europeans – so many, it might be said, that they have been trying to restore it since 1945. Already during the war, German technocrats were planning a new interdependent continental economy. Whether the benefits of continental integration and planning could ever have been separated from the political costs of terror, exploitation, and despotism is, of course, another matter. In any event, whether a victorious Hitler could have given Europe a successful Pan-European "Common Market" is an idle question. That was never Hitler's plan. To the end, he remained fixed on his vision of racist *Lebensraum*. Himmler was his lieutenant, not Schacht.

Nevertheless, it cannot be said that Hitler's vision of an autarchic German superstate failed for economic reasons. On the contrary, even the miniature autarchy of the 1930s succeeded rather better than the not dissimilar economic policies of the United States and Britain. Germany recovered from the depression much faster than they, and not merely because of rearmament. Indeed, if anything, rearmament spoiled the German recovery. Nor can it really be said that the prewar economic arrangements that Germany imposed upon its Slavic neighbors proved economically unworkable.

These conclusions lead back to more fundamental questions. Could Hitler have stopped, as Schacht and other conservatives wished? Could some more "pragmatic" leader have stabilized an autarchic Germany without a general war? Could Germany have been "appeased"? These questions, like most others that have to do with the German Problem, have an internal and and external aspect. Internally, what compulsions drove his regime? Externally, what chance had such a Germany for long-range security?

One large body of theory maintains that its very nature as a "totalitarian" regime compelled the Nazi state to ceaseless expansion. Thus, Hannah Arendt, like the conservative Rauschning, saw Hitler as a "voice of destruction," and his regime as a restless new barbarism without the moral foundations for domestic or international stability. Whatever the psychological and moral validity of this view, the economic picture does not confirm it. The Nazi domestic economy, as well as Hitler's Balkan bloc, were both relatively stable and successful – at least until rearmament began overtaxing Germany's resources. Rearmament can, of course, be seen as the outward manifestation of the inner compulsions of a totalitarian regime. Such it may have been. It was also, of course, a predictable policy for a revisionist power surrounded by traditional enemies. Rearmament had, in fact, begun under the Weimar regime, as had a revisionist foreign policy. But Hitler's goals were far more ambitious than the Little German nationalist revisionism of Weimar. There could be no lasting stability for Germany, in Hitler's view, without *Lebensraum* in the East. In theory, these bloated aims were not infinite. Germany would not reach for world power. Once achieved, the continental Third Reich was to be autarchic and inward looking. Britain would have been left alone in its empire.

But not even Chamberlain ever seriously proposed permitting Germany a continental position on such a scale. Indeed, as we note, Britain's irreconcilable opposition to the limited Balkan hegemony Germany had already achieved was a strong element in the decision to oppose Hitler over Danzig. Behind Britain, of course, lay a United State far more hostile to economic autarchy than Chamberlain's Britain. In short, given Hitler's ambitions, war was inevitable.

That a more conservative regime, without Hitler's avowed grander ambitions, would have succeeded in winning a more limited "appeasement" can hardly be taken for granted. Weimar, after all, had not got very far in pressing Germany's claims, despite considerable pro-German sympathy among the British. Once it regained its sovereignty, Germany was once more on a collision course with its neighbors. Under the circumstances, Hitler's view that the German Problem could only be resolved by war was perhaps more than just a self-fulfilling prophecy.

Hitler and His Failure

The course of Hitler's career in foreign policy hardly confirms the wisdom of either his fundamental analysis or his strategy. Like the imperial regime he had so bitterly criticized, Hitler fought his war on two fronts and lost it. While fascist Italy did become his ally, it proved a heavy liability. And Britain remained Hitler's impacable enemy. Thanks to his *Testament*, we have Hitler's own explanation of his failure, an analysis that shows the remarkable continuity of his thought.

The Italian alliance, Hitler admitted, proved to have been a bad mistake, of advantage principally to Germany's enemies. Although Hitler continued to call the Duce a perhaps even greater leader than himself, Italy's neutrality, he decided, would have been preferable to its support. As it was, Mussolini's Greek intervention required an unnecessary and costly diversion away from the Russian campaign. And Italy's old-fashioned colonial ambitions inhibited Germany from espousing the cause of anticolonialism and Moslem emancipation.

Whatever the faults of the Italians, the essential reason for his failure, as Hitler saw it, was Britain's irrational unwillingness to make peace. British intransigence robbed him of his quick victory in the West and forced his hand prematurely in Russia.

Why, in fact, did Hitler attack Russia and thus himself initiate a two-front war? A Britain under Churchill's "Jew-ridden leadership would never come to terms, he had decided, as long as the Russian card remained unplayed. So the war with Britain would never end until Russia was defeated. Moreover, with Germany's urgent need for living space and Bolshevik Russia's own fundamental ambitions and antipathies, war in the East was inevitable in any event. Both sides knew it; Stalin himself was only waiting for the favorable moment.

Not only was Russia poised to strike, according to Hitler, but the United States was also steadily moving toward war. Roosevelt's domestic program was failing, and his administration was dominated by Jewish interests. With Britain refusing to come to terms, the president would soon find a pretext for intervention. Time was not on Germany's side. As Hitler's observations imply, once the United States and Russia gathered and combined their vast resources, Germany's fate would be sealed. Hitler's victory had to come quickly, with Germany's armies fresh and ready, or it would not come at all. Russia, with its vast spaces, Slavic patience, and Marxist optimism, could endure and wait. Unlike its enemies, Hitler lamented, Germany was forever condemned to be in a hurry.

He might have won his gamble and defeated Russia in 1941, Hitler believed, had it not been for Mussolini's idiotic intervention in Greece. Rescuing Mussolini wasted precious time and resources. The Russian campaign could not be launched until June 22, and was not quite finished before the terrible winter set in. Hence, Hitler lost his great gamble against time.

Nevertheless, Britain was admittedly his major strategic miscalculation. But even with his other failings, Hitler concluded, he could not be blamed for failing to anticipate British obstinacy. He had correctly assessed the true interests of the British, he believed, but overestimated their intelligence. It was not his fault if they had chosen to destroy their own world position rather than come to terms with him. He had tried, he claimed, to make accommodation easy. He had, for example, made a gallant gesture at Dunkirk. The British proved incapable of appreciating it.

After they had defended themselves in the Battle of Britain, and defeated Italy in the Mediterranean, their overriding national interest called on them to make peace. Europe would then have been united under German hegemony; the Jewish poison would have been eradicated; and France and Italy would have been forced to renounce inappropriate aspirations to greatness. Germany, its rear secure, could have turned wholeheartedly to the fundamental objectives of its foreign policy: destroying Bolshevism and conquering wide spaces in the East. Britain, freed from European cares, could have devoted itself to empire. A new world balance would have preserved it:

If fate had granted to an aging and enfeebled Britain a new Pitt instead of this Jew-ridden, half-American drunkard, the new Pitt would at once have recognized that Britain's traditional policy of balance of power would now have to be applied on a different scale, and this time on a worldwide scale. Instead of maintaining, creating and adding fuel to European rivalries, Britain ought to do her utmost to encourage and bring about a reunification of Europe. Allied to a united Europe, she would then still retain the chance of being able to play the part of arbiter in world affairs . . .[4]
[Churchill] has made the same mistakes as those generals make who wage a war according to the principles of the preceding war. . . . The crucial new factor [since Pitt's day] is the existence of those two giants, the U.S. and Russia. Pitt's England ensured the balance of world power by preventing the hegemony of Europe – by preventing Napoleon, that is, from attaining his goal. Churchill's England, on the other hand, should have allowed the unification of Europe, if it wished to preserve that same balance of power.[5]

Hitler concluded in 1945: "We can with safety make one prophecy: whatever the outcome of this war, the British Empire is at an end. It has been mortally wounded. The future of the British people is to die of hunger and tuberculosis on their cursed island."[6] "Churchill, by refus-

---

[4] Hitler, *The Testament of Adolf Hitler*, p. 32.
[5] Ibid., p. 30.
[6] Ibid., p. 34.

ing to come to terms with me, has condemned his country to a policy of suicide."[7] Americans, Russians, and Jews would emerge the war's great victors. Americans and Russians would soon contest the globe. The Jews, in their arrogance, would ultimately overextend themselves. Germany, although its sufferings would be great in defeat, was fundamentally healthy, Hitler decided. The German people, purged of their Jews, would revive. Hitler summarized the future thus:

. . . with the defeat of the Reich and pending the emergence of the Asiatic, the African and, perhaps, the South American nationalisms, there will remain in the world only two Great Powers capable of confronting each other – the United States and Soviet Russia. The laws of both history and geography will compel these two Powers to a trial of strength, either military or in the field of economics and ideology. These same laws make it inevitable that both Powers should become enemies of Europe. And it is equally certain that both these Powers will sooner or later find it desirable to seek the support of the sole surviving great nation in Europe, the German people. I say with all the emphasis at my command that the Germans must at all costs avoid playing the role of pawn in either camp.[8]

Sitting in his bunker, Hitler speculated on what would happen to Europe. He wondered if he had not been the old Continent's last chance. Europe was incapable of voluntary reform, he decided. A new Europe could be built only upon the ruins of all those vested interests – economic coalitions, mental rigidities, narrow and perverse prejudices – that preserved a decrepit status quo. Napoleon had understood this and had longed for a stable peace, Hitler judged. But, like Hitler, he had been compelled forever to wage war:

And always it has been this Britain who barred Europe's way to prosperity. But now she is aged and enfeebled, though not less vicious and wicked. Finally, she is being supported in this negative and unnatural attitude by the United States, themselves inspired and

[7] Ibid., p. 30.
[8] Ibid., pp. 107–8.

urged on by the whole forces of international Jewry, which has flourished and hopes long to continue to flourish as a result of our dissensions.[9]

The United States, itself, would eventually go under, Hitler believed, if it did not shake off the domination of the Jews. With its vast resources and equally vast unintelligence, the United States seemed to him like "some child stricken with elephantiasis."[10] Should it collapse, a great new opportunity would open to the yellow races. In this new and supremely dangerous world, only those white races would survive who had learned to be strong and courageous in suffering and had eradicated from themselves the deadly poison of Jewry. Thus, Hitler's valedictory hopes for Germany. As for the Jews: "[In victory] they will become so arrogant that they will evoke a violent reaction against them. . . . The shifty, the shamefaced Jew will disappear and will be replaced by a Jew vainglorious and bombastic. . . . There is, then, no danger in the circumstances that anti-Semitism will disappear, for it is the Jews themselves who add fuel to its flames and see that it is kept well stoked."[11]

Hitler's Analysis Reconsidered:
The Failure with Britain

Hitler's explanation of his own downfall, and its future consequences, exhibits his characteristic combination of shrewdness, viciousness, and logical extremism. His fundamental argument, that Britain ruined itself and Europe by not coming to terms with Germany, is, of course, a variation on an old theme in English as well as German politics. Since the later nineteenth century, British strategists had talked of an Anglo-German accommodation to avoid

[9] Ibid., p. 102.
[10] Ibid., p. 108.
[11] Ibid., pp. 52–3.

mutual ruin and help contain the rising power of the United States. Various initiatives toward Germany were essayed, most notably by Joseph Chamberlain in 1898. In retrospect at least, such a strategy for Britain has a plausible appeal. Certainly, for all its glorious courage, Britain emerged in many ways the loser from the Second World War, if not indeed from the First. The United States has gradually taken over Britain's old world-economic position, and Britain has found it increasingly difficult even to keep up with those powers who were ostensibly defeated – France, Germany, and Japan.

Why, in 1938 or 1941, did the British reject any German deal out of hand? Why did they choose instead to pursue a war that predictably led to the ruin of their imperial position?

It may be useful to speculate on various explanations. Hitler, of course, blamed the Jews. But even if their influence was considerable, Hitler could hardly have expected them to embrace him. Hitler also blamed Churchill. Perhaps Churchill was too pugnaciously stubborn for Britain's long-range interest. Or perhaps he was predisposed toward a policy of devolving Britain's imperial position to America with the hope that an Anglo-American special relationship might safeguard Britain's prosperity and influence. Certainly, from the late nineteenth century on, many Britishers have seen American ascendancy as the most natural and desirable evolution for the world political-economic system that they originally created. These same people, having convinced themselves of the necessity of a hegemonic power to manage the world, and realizing their own incapacity to continue the role, were content to play Greece to the new American Rome. The United States was, after all, a branch from Britain's political tree.

Such views may have been widely held, but not by Britain's government in the late 1930s. Chamberlain was in power, not Churchill, and Chamberlain was both acutely

sensitive about the threat to Britain from America's economic ascendency and highly skeptical about expecting to
protect Britain's interests through partnership with the
United States. Yet Chamberlain was scarcely more willing
than Churchill to accept Hitler's terms for a general settlement. As the guarantee to Poland made clear, Britain
would not give Germany a free hand in the East. Throughout the thirties, in fact, Britain stoutly resisted German
economic expansion in the Balkans, despite the relatively
trivial economic significance of the area for Britain —
particularly by comparison with its commercial interests
in Germany itself.

Why the unwillingness to conciliate? Perhaps the British
were simply too greedy. The lure of Balkan oil and finance
may have been sufficiently appealing in every instance to
frustrate initiatives toward a global settlement. In the
1920s, after all, the British had quarreled furiously with
the French over Eastern European finances. Enmity with
France, nurtured in contests so irrelevant to Britain's wider
interests, probably cost Britain a good deal as the pound
grew weak in the later twenties.

One cause is obvious. The British public despised and
feared Hitler. The Nazi political system, although impressive for its quick economic results, was repugnant to liberal sensitivities, quite apart from the special antipathies
of the Jews or the Marxists. And Hitler's diplomatic style
scarcely improved Germany's international reputation. The
British Empire, to be sure, had not been forged by men
who allowed their sensitivity about the domestic or foreign
manners of their allies to prejudice Britain's vital interests.
But Hitler placed excessive demands on even the most ruthless parliamentary leader.

Sorting out these various ideological and personal considerations in British policy is interesting, but also probably irrelevant. For whatever the motives, conscious or
unconscious, Britain's rejection of German ambitions had

a justification cold-blooded enough for Hitler himself to understand, and indeed to expect. In the deal that Hitler professed to have offered, Germany was to become a continental superpower at the expense of Russian territory and French pretensions. Britain was to be left undisturbed in its empire and would secure, from a German-dominated Europe, a counterweight and potential ally against the United States' otherwise overweening world power. A dispassionate British policy, sensitive to the dangers of American preponderance and prepared to ignore Hitler's domestic horrors, would nevertheless ultimately reject such an arrangement. For how could the British be expected to gamble their future on the assumption that Hitler's German superstate would remain peacefully autarchic? What was to prevent Germany from expanding its commercial and military reach outward once the vast continental bastion was secure? To begin with, why should the British trust Hitler? Despite his clarity in *Mein Kampf* and the *Secret Book*, his later pronouncements were ambiguous. Although he ostensibly rejected a German world-economic role for the present, Hitler clearly wanted Germany to be a major world force. And his dynamic and competitive view of history belied any static assignment of roles. In any event, regardless of Hitler's momentary intentions, was it plausible to expect a nation with Germany's extraordinary commercial and industrial dynamism to remain uninterested in the world economy? Who could guarantee that a German superpower would not imitate the United States? A vast continental system would be the protected base from which German economic power would project itself into the world at large. Britain, having sacrificed its continental allies and spurned American friendship, would then have been left to face an infinitely stronger and more ruthless version of the old Imperial Germany. In effect, Hitler's ambition and the threat of war confronted the British with the choice between two masters. They would have preferred, of course, to avoid the choice altogether, but Hitler's dynamic expansion made temporizing impossible. Not surprisingly, in the end they chose Roosevelt's America over Hitler's Germany.

As Hitler's own view of the world ought to have made clear to him, no other European Great Power, Britain included, would voluntarily acquiesce in German hegemony. If Germany wanted its "living space," and the continental hegemony that was its inevitable consequence, Germany would have to win and hold it by force. Finally Hitler's Germany, like the kaiser's before him, was not strong enough for its ambitions. Quite apart from the Americans, Europe itself had too many Great Powers. A Germany seeking military hegemony could neither prevent the others from uniting against it, nor defeat them when they did.

Germany's failure, it could be argued, came not merely from a lack of strength, but from certain historic liabilities that made it particularly unsuited for a hegemonic role. The Germans have seemed particularly inept at winning allies. They have never found a way to legitimize their hegemony. True, there were promising possibilities. The notion that Europe must unite, or see itself dominated from without, might have been sufficiently obvious and compelling to stabilize German predominance, particularly after the French had been defeated. But Hitler's vision for Europe, based on his exclusive racist creed, offered little to other Europeans. If racially suitable, they might expect to become reconditioned Germans. Otherwise, they would be exterminated or enslaved. It was an unpromising program out of which to concoct an acceptable ideology—a decent drapery—to legitimize and soften German domination. As an ideology for hegemony, it scarcely compares with the liberalism of the French Revolution, the rationalism of Napoleon, or the anticommunism and economic liberalism of the postwar American system.

German clumsiness with hegemony perhaps sprang from a certain cultural inwardness. No doubt Nazism represented a peculiarly exclusive expression of German culture. But, as preceding chapters discuss, the Imperial Germans were scarcely more successful in the First World War. In neither war could the Germans develop an effective ideological foundation for their hegemony. Their shortcomings in this respect seem more a matter of psychology and manners than a lack of artistic or intellectual substance. Nineteenth-century Germany was hardly deficient in genius. But the land of Goethe, Beethoven, Hegel, and Wagner ought to have been more serene and generous in its pride. Instead, the face it turned to Europe was arrogant, embattled, and defensive. Perhaps, as Hitler sometimes said, German culture lacked the confidence to proclaim itself universal.

If the Germans were feeble in rationalizing their hegemony, they also proved inept in practicing it. To be sure, wartime occupations easily bring out the worst in everyone. And the racial policy was hardly calculated to win allies. But in neither war did the Germans collectively show much talent for managing allies. Certainly their imaginations stopped well short of that multilateral hocus-pocus characteristic of postwar American hegemony.

Hitler's Analysis Reconsidered: The Future of Europe

Hitler proved perhaps a better analyst of the world after his death than before. With his defeat, Britain soon faded and Europe was partitioned between the superpowers. As Europe's major states recovered, they once again worried about their future in a world of giants. The old fear suggested the old solution: unity. With Germany truncated, Britain declining, and France rising, the major states were probably more equal than ever. None was an obvious candidate for hegemony. Moreover, America's protectorate and

Russia's threat limited their room for maneuver. Under the circumstances, the old impulse toward union looked to some form of federalism. The result has been a sort of European coalition organized around the Common Market. Its rationale is not unfamiliar to students of the German Problem. An integrated economy is expected to give Europe the scale to compete with the United States. Collective European strength exerted in the world outside is to defend Europe's physical and economic security. As the strongest state with the most dynamic economy, Germany might be expected to benefit the most. The whole arrangement thus answers that geopolitical concern that has troubled Germans throughout this century. It offers something for everyone. For the idealist, union overcomes Europe's weakness through peaceful cooperation, without crushing the independence of smaller states or leading to a fight to the death among the greater. For the cynic, union represents a more imaginative and effective way to establish the hegemony of the strongest. Had the Germans possessed such political grace and guile earlier in the century, one might say, Europe and the world might have been spared a great deal of turmoil.

In his fashion, Hitler considered this option and rejected it completely. The reasons are significant. His views can be found in his scathing comments about Stresemann and the brief Franco-German entente of the late twenties, and, above all, in his discussion of "Pan-Europa" in the *Secret Book* of 1928. All Europe, he noted, would share Germany's fate in the coming brutal economic competition with America:

It is frivolous . . . to believe that the contest between Europe and America will always be only of a peaceful economic nature, if economic motives develop into determining vital factors . . . [As America's internal colonisation comes to a close . . .] the natural, activist urge that is peculiar to young nations will turn outward. But then the surprises which the world may perchance still experience could least of all be seriously opposed by a pacifistic-democratic Pan-European hodge-podge state.[12]

The credulous might conclude that Europe, to prepare itself, had to form a union like the United States. But America's strength, Hitler argued, came from a long process of unification. No mechanical European coalition could expect to mobilize comparable strength merely by adding together comparable numbers. Unification in Europe would exhaust its whole strength with internal rivalries. But even achieving hegemony in a cosmopolitan Europe would be self-defeating for the victor. For the dominant state would soon submerge its race and disappear.

It was, in effect, the cosmopolitanism of Pan-Europa that outraged Hitler. Jews would welcome it, he noted. They would flourish while other peoples lost their identities and governments. Such an idea of Europe was, as he saw it, the rebirth on a grand scale of the old Austria – that "liveliest example of the enormous strength of structures artificially glued together"[13] Coudenhove Kalergi, a Hungarian nobleman who was Pan-Europa's tireless promoter, was for Hitler "everybody's bastard," who foolishly imagined a Pan-Europa someday playing "the same role vis-à-vis the American union or a nationally awakened China that was formerly played by the old Austrian state vis-à-vis Germany or Russia."[14] For Hitler, Pan-Europa was the old Habsburg monster coming back to life: "It is the rootless spirit of the imperial city of Vienna, that hybrid city of the Orient and the Occident, which thereby appeals to us."[15]

Hitler's scorn was far more than the usual nationalist skepticism about the viability of multinational states. For he not only dismissed the notion of a confederal Europe not based on domination, but he feared even more the con-

[12] Adolf Hitler, *Hitler's Secret Book* (New York: Grove Press, 1961), p. 107.
[13] Ibid., p. 108.
[14] Ibid., p. 107.
[15] Ibid., p. 108.

sequences of domination, should Germany achieve it. For victory would trap the Germans, just as they had been ensnared by the old Austrian Empire. They would gradually be absorbed by their conquests and ultimately disappear into a sort of "race trap." Hitler's arguments against Pan-Europa bring us to the same point we had reached earlier: Hitler's racism left no room for other people in his European superstate, not even as tributaries. To observe that the race policy was fatally impolitic or seriously interfered with conducting the war is to miss the point. Racial policy was the object of the war.

In summary, Hitler's territorial solution to the German Problem flowed with terrible logic, not merely from that geopolitical analysis that he shared with his imperial predecessors, but also from his own peculiar racist doctrine. The two sources were self-defeating. Those who would have agreed with his need for a strong Europe, and perhaps even accepted German hegemony to get it, found no real place in his racist scheme. His resolution of the German Problem was to annihilate Europe's other nations. Fortunately, the Germans were too weak to win alone. And thanks to Hitler's defeat, Pan-Europa, the option that he so violently rejected, was to become perhaps the principal hope for resolving the German Problem in the postwar era.

Conclusion: Hitler, Evolution or Catastrophe?

This chapter began by raising the question of Hitler's continuity with the German past. In foreign policy, the similarities between imperial and Nazi Germany are manifest. Hitler shared the same geopolitical analysis: the same certainty about conflict among nations, the same craving and rationale for hegemony over Europe. The First World War, he could claim, only sharpened the validity of that geopolitical analysis. The experience had destroyed the last illusions about European hegemony achieved peacefully or a world struggle with Britain sublimated into commercial rivalry. Germany's neighbors would never allow it to find its place peacefully. On the other hand, Hitler's bloodthirsty racism was certainly not part of Bethmann-Hollweg's vision, nor even of William II's. Racist views were easily found in Imperial Germany, but they never came to dominate any government's foreign or domestic policy. Can we therefore assume that Hitler's racism was something alien to the Germans? Was it, as is sometimes suggested, an exotic import from decadent and unhappy Austria? Were Hitler's views on the German Problem, in fact, more Austrian than German?

Such a problem is difficult to define, let alone answer. Certainly Hitler's writings give the impression that the experiences that formed his anti-Semitic creed came from his early days in Vienna, and it is easy to imagine hatred of Jews and Slavs festering in the ambience of the Dual Monarchy's disappointed and beleaguered German small bourgeoisie. Racism, of course, existed in Germany proper, as indeed it did in all other European countries. But so all-consuming a preoccupation with race seems more compatible, it can be argued, with the political culture of polyglot Austria, rather than national Germany.

Against this view, it must be noted how easily many in Germany acquiesced to Hitler's anti-Semitism – and some with much more than indifference. Indeed, Hitler's racism seems not so much an alien import as an extreme version of the general inwardness of German culture, as well as of the heavy-handedness of German rule over foreigners. If the truth be told, the Germans had never shown much capacity for cosmopolitan appeal or multinational management. Their lack of talent in this regard had gravely handicapped their foreign policy. To do it justice, Habsburg Austria was far more skillful in the practice of hegemony – perhaps because it was never ruled by its Hitlers. For all their faults, the Habsburg ruling classes were not adventurers who took their civilizing traditions lightly. Nor were they provincial nationalist bigots, unable to tolerate, respect, and accommodate other cultures. In this sense, it may be nearer the truth to say that Hitler, like his Prussian predecessors, failed because he was too much a German and not enough an Austrian. Pan-Europa doubtless did spring from Vienna. But Vienna had an older civilization with a richer political experience than Berlin. The Habsburg Empire occupies a longer and more honorable place in history than either the Second or Third Reich.

6

The German Problem: Social and Cultural Explanations

Pitfalls of Domestic Explanations

Finding the key to the German Problem in the country's domestic character has been a major preoccupation of postwar studies. The approach has several advantages not necessarily tied to its merits. For foreigners, blaming Germany's crimes on the inherent shortcomings of its society and culture is not only plausible but convenient. And for some Germans and ex-Germans, arrogating to Germany the responsibility for the century's major catastrophes justifies a certain traditional self-preoccupation and ignorance of other societies. Nevertheless, despite the convenience all around, attempts to define and relate these supposedly inherent shortcomings do not always stand up well to fair-minded examination. Often a series of stereotypes is patched up into a collective German "character." The result seems a composite projection of those qualities that people dislike most about their own societies. In many instances, the characteristics seem misinterpreted in their German context and, moreover, are easily found in other societies. At their worst, such attempts at definition seem

123

reminiscent of the very racist techniques made notorious by anti-Semites. Many worthy scholars have permitted themselves this dangerous indulgence. Although more vicious forms of anti-German propaganda are no longer fashionable among serious scholars, the effects of this defamation linger, as a certain tendency toward German baiting in contemporary Europe illustrates. Many of us, if we are honest, carry such a view of Germans just beneath the level of articulate consciousness.

The famous British historian, Sir Lewis Namier, gives a good example in a 1947 review of A. J. P. Taylor's *Course of German History*. Namier faulted Taylor for not carrying his "brilliant analysis" to the real German question: "Why do individual Germans in non-German surroundings become useful, decent citizens, but in groups develop tendencies which make them a menace to their fellowmen?" "We call the German 'inhuman': for sometimes he behaves like a beast, and sometimes like a robot. He is educated but not civilized."[1] Namier went on to provide a sketch of his own psychological and sociological explanation. Germans were isolated and tense, without grace or ease, suspiciously concerned with virility – in general, men with poor human contacts. Because their social intercourse was never natural, they required codes and rulebooks for all human relationships, even tyranny and mass murder. Among a people so inept at social communion, political creations were inevitably inorganic, incapable of spontaneous adjustment, and essentially grotesque. But whatever their shortcomings, Sir Lewis noted, Germans had a cold tenacity and bitter intensity. Once merely comic, since Bismarck they had directed their tensions into an immense drive to power. But every accession to power had only made them more frantically envious of those who possessed the "unbought grace of life," whereas every obstacle

[1] Sir Lewis Namier, *Facing East: Essays on Germany, the Balkans, and Russia in the Twentieth Century* (New York: Harper & Row, 1947), p. 21.

in their path had filled them with venomous rage. Frustration had finally driven them into a colossal doctrinaire totalitarianism: ". . . from introverse isolation they plunged into the heat and intoxication of undifferentiated, uncritical mass-hysteria."[2]

Namier, a Jew originally from Central Europe, may doubtless be forgiven for writing in such a fashion so soon after Hitler's demise. No one can deny that Nazi Germany was abominable, at home and abroad. But to lay its evils to the autonomous evolution of some innate German badness is not a satisfactory explanation. To explain that Germans behave like beasts because they are beasts is, at best, a circular confusion of causes and consequences. All societies, in fact, have innate vicious tendencies, usually restrained by a civilized veneer of mutually reinforcing ideals and inhibitions. In every society, that civilized crust has its cracks – its characteristic bigotries, class conflicts, racism, and xenophobia. In any society intense pressure can break the crust and let loose the demons. The breaks, when they come, naturally tend to run along the existing fault lines. But the breaks are a consequence not of some spontaneous widening of the cracks, but of the general build-up of pressure. To be sure, every country has its own peculiar pathology. The breakdowns of societies, like those of individuals, reveal idiosyncratic perversions as well as general symptoms. Everyone goes mad in his own fashion. But madness is more usually the consequence rather than the explanation of the breakdown.

The same point applies to nations. Many studies have sought to trace the roots of the Nazi madness deep into traditional German society and culture. The roots are no doubt there, and the studies teach us many things, but they do not in themselves explain the deadly flower. And if the lesson we draw is the wickedness of Germans rather than the faults of man, we convert tragedy into ideology and

2 Ibid., p. 23.

mock the sufferings of a whole generation. For despite all the studies of the Nazi era, studies indeed that begin to constitute a sort of popular political pornography, it cannot be established that Germany was inherently more prone to wickedness than other Western nations. Instead it was a country whose geographical and historical circumstances subjected it to pressure too intense for its political structure and civilized elites to control. Once the breakdown had occurred, and a resourceful and unscrupulous tyranny was installed, Germans became the slaves of their own worst instincts. But even this Germany ought not to be seen as a monster, but as a country whose horrifying modern history holds lessons for us all.

Such a broad caveat cannot, of course, be "proved" in so general a form. But it can be illustrated in detail. Perhaps it would be useful, therefore, to take a look at three topics commonly treated in most contemporary analyses of traditional German culture: Germany's "atavistic feudal" elites, traditional anti-Semitism, and "apolitical" philosophical tradition. All three have often been treated as inherent and unique German social and cultural deformations. All three notions, I expect, are in need of certain skeptical revision. My brief observations cannot hope to do justice to the broad issues involved, but may at least suggest some lines for revising overworked stereotypes, as well as sketch the relationship between Germany's domestic developments and a broader view of the German Problem.

Germany's Atavistic Elites

One of the most popular theories about modern German society blames many of its problems on a persisting predominance of "precapitalist" elites. As noted in Chapter 4, an entire school of analysts bases itself of hypothesis – a school that owes much to Veblen, received its definitive expression from Schumpeter, was further developed and popularized by Gerschenkron and Barrington Moore, and today power-fully influences the writings of many German historians. Schumpeter was trying to explain why wars, presumably irrational economically, nevertheless persisted in a capitalist system. Schumpeter found the answer in the sociology of modernization rather than the economics of capitalism. Economic rationalization, Schumpeter noted, threatened privileged feudal classes in both their traditional political function and their agricultural economic base. A rational market fated them for "creative destruction" – to use one of Schumpeter's more striking phrases. The underbrush of the feudal era was to be cleared away to make room for the fresh growth of capitalism. But in many societies, the market was not allowed to do its work. A feckless bourgeoisie was too preoccupied with short-term profit, or too dazzled by aristocratic prestige, to take political control and orient policy toward the peaceful goals appropriate to a rational modern economy. Thus, the old elites were able to use their political connections and skills to manipulate modernization toward mercantilism, imperialism, and war. Imperialist mercantilism perversely oriented economic life toward power rather than profit. Hence the continuing need for armies, fleets, colonies, and all the rest of the imperialist paraphernalia, including the military elites themselves. Hence, too, the military justification for preserving uncompetitive feudal agriculture. For Schumpeter, Germany was a prime example. An agrarian elite continued to dominate politically an advanced capitalist economy. The result was agricultural and industrial protectionism and a mercantilist, power-oriented view of trade, competition, and business organization. These economically irrational perspectives fed a German imperialist drive toward colonialism and European hegemony.

With so distinguished a band of adherents, the theory is obviously attractive. Unfortunately, in the presumably rather significant case of the First World War, the theory does not appear to apply very well. Indeed it seems almost to invert reality completely. As Chapter 3 argues, the decisive cause of the First World War was the inability of Germany and Britain to come to terms on either a European or an international order. As chapter 4 points out, their conflict had little to do with Junker grain tariffs, but a great deal to do with Germany's naval and commercial challenge to Britain. Neither challenge, nor imperialism generally, can reasonably be laid to "atavistic" Junker interests or causes.

Kehr's exploration of the all-important fleet question brings out these points clearly. The Junker agrarians and their political representatives were not enthusiastic about territorial expansion. On the contrary, they had always opposed a Big Germany, both because it would diminish the relative political weight of Prussia, which was their political base, and also because it would bring powerful agricultural competition inside the Reich. At home, the Junkers were mostly concerned with their gradual decline in the face of a rapidly modernizing captalist society; abroad they feared the military threat from France and Russia and the economic threat from Russian agriculture. Junkers thus had little interest in an expansionist world policy that would increase still further the already overwhelming weight of German industry. As Kehr saw it, the Junkers really yearned for an agricultural Prussia that bought its manufactures from Britain. Left to their own devices, they would have sacrificed the protectionist and expansionist interests of German industry for an alliance with Britain against France and Russia. Such a policy, however, would have been outrageously incompatible with the dynamic thrust of an already industrial Germany. The Junkers knew they could never carry it. They themselves were caught in a fatal contradiction. For their extreme agrarian policy would have denied Germany the industrial base for a modern army, that Prussian army which was the Junker's special preserve and justification. So the Junkers made the best deal they could. They reluctantly supported the imperialism of big business in return for enough agricultural protection to preserve their own economic base.

The Junkers, it bears noting, were slowly losing control of the army. A modern mass army could not officer itself exclusively from the old military classes. Reluctantly but increasingly, the Junker officer yielded to the bourgeois officer. That these middle-class officers often became parodies of Junker sensibilities was an understandable social phenomenon, demonstrating not so much the Junker's domination as his appropriation. It was the newly arrived bourgeois warriors, by the way, who introduced a particularly shameful anti-Semitism into the officer corps.

For all their social prestige, the Junkers did not dominate policy in late Imperial Germany. Old political forms persisted, in particular the monarchy and the weighted Prussian suffrage, but the middle class was clearly in the ascendancy. The Hohenzollern crown had more sense than to make itself dependent on the Junkers. The kaiser, with his rabid support for naval and economic imperialism, tried to make the monarchy the spokesman for the most powerful and dynamic of the country's economic and social forces. Under the circumstances, the Junkers could flourish only insofar as they reconciled themselves with the requirements of a rapidly modernizing society. If they learned to be imperialists, it was to fit those requirements. In short, it was the big bourgeoisie who were ascendant in Imperial Germany, as in every other modern country. It was they who built Germany into a giant export machine, challenging Britain throughout the globe. It was Krupp's ravenous steel mills that financed the Navy League, and profited most from the fleet. It was the imperialist aggressiveness and anxiety of the dominant bourgeois class that was responsible for the conflict with Britain and, increasingly, for the conflict with a rapidly industrializing Russia as well.

That Schumpeter and his academic followers should

blame the Junkers for German imperialism is not without irony. For among the most imperialist and warlike groups in German society were bourgeois professors, Protestant clergy, and the intellectuals generally. Generalizations about intellectuals are doubtless even more hazardous than about "atavistic elites." But it was the middle-class intellectuals who provided and often popularized the economic and historic rationale for imperialist expansion. It was they who nourished and legitimized Pan-Germanism and at least the more sophisticated versions of anti-Semitism. As bourgeois industry rejoiced in the power of science to manipulate nature, so the bourgeois intellectual played with the power of ideas over a mass society.

Schumpeter's approach gains plausibility by focusing on the undeniably militaristic tone of Wilhelmine Germany's political culture. The style of Imperial Germany's politics, diplomacy, and indeed commerce were heavily infused with the militaristic ethos associated with Prussia. Thus, it can be claimed, even if the Junkers were losing their real power, their lingering cultural, intellectual, and social hegemony dominated the perspectives of the rising bourgeoisie. Perhaps. But adopting aristocratic manners does not necessarily mean abandoning bourgeois interests, in Germany any more than in Britain or France. In the Victorian Compromise, the aristocracy may have survived but it was the bourgeoisie who triumphed.

Kehr, I believe, offers a more promising approach. German militarism was, he found, itself a reflection of an all-prevailing materialism in the German political culture of the time. The Left embraced Marx's economic determinism; the Right turned to a materialism of power: "They had in common their unspiritual, materialistic base and the idea that everything else should be only superstructure."[3] Even socialists, Kehr argues, inclined toward the imperial-

[3] Eckart Kehr, *Battleship Building and Party Politics in Germany 1894–1901* (1930) (Chicago: University of Chicago Press, 1973), p. 430.

ist view that economic development depended ultimately upon state power. Behind the preoccupation with power was loss of faith in a rational universe:

The destruction of natural law in Germany by Hegel had left after his death only a brutal philosophy of power as an ideological frame without content. . . . The lack of original ideas – in a future history of political theory only an empty page can be devoted to the period of the German empire – and of political understanding of the internal as well as of the external position of the empire, the armaments policy and the spiritual desiccation of the nation are inextricably interwoven correlatives.[4]

Hence, Kehr continued, not only the mindless emptiness of German policy, but its particularly repellent quality for other states. Germany failed to provide a convincing ethical justification of its power. German ideology "was not sufficiently permeated with culture and morality to educate the nation in foreign policy to the use of cant in the grand manner. . . ."[5]

It is possible, of course to quarrel with Kehr's use of the term materialism, and the way he opposes it to natural law. Marx too has "laws," springing inevitably from his materialist conception of nature. Marx did, however, teach that ideals were a "superstructure" – an "ideology" to justify "real," that is to say, material interests. In any event, Kehr's basic point about the imperialists that their enthusiasm for power was an "ideological frame without content" seems sound enough. Kehr found the imperial era a remarkably uncreative age in the world of ideas – a blank page in political theory. But in retrospect, two major intellectual figures from this period do come to mind – Nietzsche and Max Weber. Although neither was an enthusiast of the imperial regime, and neither, in my view, can exactly be called a "materialist," each in his fashion saw a world shaped by power rather than law. Nietzsche's aes-

4 Ibid., pp. 444–5.
5 Ibid., p. 434.

thetic voluntarism and contempt for natural law are obvious. And Weber, for all his emphasis on rationality in domestic society, was a tough-minded imperialist abroad, who found no principle for the international system other than the clash of great modern states for world supremacy.

Hegel, Nietzsche, and Weber – not to mention Wagner, Marx, and Darwin himself – were all bourgeois. Their worldview cannot plausibly be traced to the prestige of Prussian Junkers. What Kehr calls materialism, the view of Nature as indifferent toward humane values, a view that made civilization a contrivance of human will, was common in all national cultures of the late nineteenth century. The imperialist corollary, derived from a Nature "red in tooth and claw," was hardly limited to Germany. Materialism and imperialism were general cosmopolitan features of later nineteenth-century bourgeois culture. Under the circumstances, the picture of Imperial Germany developed in Allied propaganda, and reflected ever afterward in Allied scholarship, seems suspiciously like a projection onto the Germans of that power-hungry materialism characteristic of nineteenth-century culture everywhere. The Germans, of course, helped their own defamation. Their nationalism was irritatingly crude and bombastic. Junker soldiers and landlords were perhaps not so cultivated models for middle-class imitation as the English gentry. And, as Kehr notes, the peculiar weakness of a natural-law tradition in Germany, thanks to Hegel and Marx, hampered German politicians in developing cant to the high art that it became in late Victorian England. Yet were these deficiencies so significant? Were the Germans more aggressive or militarist than the British and French who between them had annexed the better part of the world? To be sure, German industry was outward-thrusting. But was British industry any less so?

In summary, the Schumpeter thesis, convenient as it is, tends to distort the facts of German imperialism. Late nineteenth-century imperialism in Germany, and doubtless else-where, arose not from the remnants of "feudalism," as Schumpeter has it, but from the avant garde of an infinitely expansive capitalism. "Irrational" forces did not smother capitalism; capitalism itself had ceased to be "rational" in classic market terms. In the leading industries, power and organization had long since transformed the simple market models based on comparative advantage. Because the benefits of technology and organization were thought to be unlimited, nature was thought to be infinitely malleable to human will. Imperialism was the expression in the international political arena of a Faustian fascination with unlimited power and growth, a symptom of the general loss of measure that has afflicted all modern societies. That Faustian lust after infinity is perhaps the principal theme running through modern bourgeois culture. It is truly a bourgeois disease, not to be blamed on a group of declining East Elbian grain farmers, selling their fading political influence to stretch out a traditional way of life.

Anti-Semitism

No one can study modern German culture without confronting the racial crimes of the Nazi era. If German political culture is not uniquely and profoundly flawed, how can the cold-blooded murder of six million Jews be explained? Nazi Germany's murder of the Jews was an appalling historical crime, which should bring deep shame to the generations responsible. Not, of course, that Germany is the only Western nation burdened with horrors; most have an impressive catalogue of barbarities against other peoples. The British have Ireland and India. The United States has its thousands of massacred Indians and Filipinos, not to mention the degradation and brutality of black slavery that even now numbs the imagination. Indeed, not many years ago, we found ourselves systematically using the most infernal modern weapons to destroy civilian villages in Indochina. None of this is any excuse for the Nazis. But at the very least, it suggests the universality and complexity of evil.

Nevertheless, the question remains. Why the Holocaust? I cannot even pretend to answer in any comprehensive way so complex and painful a question here. But perhaps it will be useful to suggest a broader approach to the nature of anti-Semitism, an approach that makes it less incongruous, if no less revolting – an approach that perhaps just begins to be possible after thirty postwar years.

Germans have understandably sought to blame the Holocaust on Hitler rather than on Germany. Hitler's rise, policies, and theories have all been discussed above. Hitler came to power when German society was under intense economic pressure, and after a long period of national humiliation and disorientation. That Germany should have turned to a dictator was not surprising. That Hitler's early economic and diplomatic successes should have won support and weakened opposition was not surprising either – particularly when success was combined with a mastery of demagogic propaganda and ruthless terror. Hitler's personal anti-Semitism has often been explained. It was not rare among men of his background and experience. Harder to explain is how presumably decent Germans, the conservative elites in particular, actually assisted the Nazis to power and thereafter condoned or at least remained passive before the stupefying evil that unfolded. What strange moral obtuseness made them unable to realize that such uninhibited criminality, visible above all in the Jewish policies, would ultimately destroy the society that harbored it?

The subject has been analyzed endlessly. Trying to assay the significance of anti-Semitism in popular or elite support for Hitler runs up against both the difficulty of assessing public opinion in a dictatorship, and of isolating one factor in that opinion from many others. Numerous extenuating circumstances are often cited. Wholesale extermination came only toward the war's end, when public opinion was throttled and resistance inhibited. Moreover, the treatment of the Jews should not be taken out of its broader context, it is said. Hundreds of thousands of other Germans were also in concentration camps; many millions of Slavs were exterminated along with the Jews. Although these points doubtless give a more complete view, they can hardly be said to exonerate German honor, in particular that of the conservative elites. It was those elites, after all, incarnated by Hindenburg and Papen, who brought Hitler to power. It seems unlikely that they willed what was to happen to the Jews, or even approved of the virulence of Hitler's earlier anti-Semitism. But German conservatives had grown callous about anti-Semitism because they themselves had long carried on a flirtation with its demonic political force. The reasons go back to the relatively civilized society of Bismarckian times. The explanation is found less in any inherent racism among conservative elites than in the political configuration that took form with the democratization of Imperial German politics. Among these elites, anti-Semitism was more a question of power than of race. Such an explanation, although it does not lessen the crime, at least makes its motive seem more credible.

In the late nineteenth century, anti-Semitism was familiar everywhere in Europe. East of Germany, it was far worse. By contrast with Imperial Russia, Germans were tolerance itself. Indeed, a survey of Western societies around the time of the Dreyfus Affair would have been unlikely to single out either Germany or Austria as particularly infected. In both societies exceptional Jews had achieved great wealth and power, and many more had begun to occupy prominent places in the professions. Some prominent families of Jewish origin had "assimilated" to Christianity. Some did not, like Bismarck's banker, Gerson

Bleichröder, who nevertheless had become a Prussian noble in the 1870s.

Despite the widespread progress of Jews in Bismarckian Germany, prejudice against them was common. It was doubtless as unattractive, stupid, and painful as snobbery can be, but it was very different from that deliberate stimulation of anti-Semitic hatred among the masses that came to Germany during the 1880s and intermittently thereafter. This politically organized anti-Semitism, even if it did not stop the rapid rise of German Jews, and was no worse than in France, nevertheless increasingly wounded, alienated, and embittered the Jews while it coarsened and brutalized German society in general. Again, how can this political anti-Semitism be explained? Why did supposedly decent elements of German society tolerate it? While competition and arriviste snobbery may explain anti-Semitism among some of the new middle classes, why were the conservative agrarian parties, representatives of the older landed elites, so strongly attracted toward it?

A sensitive study of the Jews among the Imperial German elites emerges from Fritz Stern's recent biography of Bismarck's banker, Gerson Bleichröder. Bleichröder's rise from the ghetto was astonishing. He began as a small banker running errands for the Rothschilds. By the 1870s the House of Bleichröder had become a major European bank and Bleichröder's own wealth was thought to be matched only by Krupp's. In 1872, William I made Bleichröder a Prussian noble. Bleichröder owed his rise not only to talent and Rothschild patronage, but to his close relationship with Bismarck. The Iron Chancellor, thanks to the kaiser's munificence and his own prudent management, had gradually become a big Prussian landowner with substantial portfolio investments. Bismarck took great interest in his possessions. Bleichröder was his manager and constant adviser. Bleichröder extended his advice to general economic questions and, in turn, served as a conduit to the financial world. He helped raise the funds that permitted Bismarck to defy Parliament in the 1860s, and he served as Bismarck's agent in a wide variety of confidential and covert matters in Germany and abroad. In particular, Bleichröder managed and was intimately involved in the distribution of Bismarck's discretionary political funds. Stern's study of Bleichröder's activities thus lights up the whole underworld of Bismarck's power.

Bleichröder had many virtues appropriate for a great private banker – prudence, financial integrity, discretion, and often unusual solicitude and kindness for his clients. He also closely approximated the classic stereotype of a climbing nouveau riche. He was painfully eager to be accepted in high German society, and consequently was a snob, toady, and general busybody. His opulent hospitality and generous presents were both enjoyed and despised by their aristocratic recipients. His closeness to Bismarck's covert power, and his reputation as a manipulator and wire-puller, made many contemporaries suspicious and fearful. In fact, Bleichröder was accepted well enough – all things considered – by the Court and by Berlin society in general. His usefulness, prudence, and anxious kindness were appreciated, even if he was made fun of behind his back and occasionally treated rudely to his face. Such, after all, is the lot of most successful climbers. Whether the enormous effort was worth it, or whether Bleichröder died with his mouth full of ashes, as Stern deftly suggests, is one of those existential questions that form the stuff of human drama. The same question, after all, could be asked about the haunted and hysterical Bismarck. In any event, even if Bleichröder had been a model of sophisticated restraint, he would have been disliked for his great new wealth.

As Germany rapidly transformed itself into a modern industrial society, traditional classes naturally felt themselves losing their social control and personal security. Power was passing to the new men who knew how to manipulate new forces and techniques. To the landed elites, industrialists seemed bad enough. But bankers and stockbrokers were counted particularly anathema – wire-pullers abstracted from the realities of social leadership or genuine production, parasites feeding on the misfortunes of worthy people entrapped in the sophistry of modern finance. Many of the traditional aristocratic and bourgeois elites had, in fact, greedily plunged into unwise speculation and been badly hurt, especially by the crash of 1873. Like most people, they wanted things both ways. They wanted new wealth and ancient prestige. In the new imperial world, many were slipping on both counts. To such people, Bleichröder, the most successful of the great private bankers, easily became a hated symbol.

That he was a Jew merely embellished his symbolic role. He would have been hated anyway. He was hated all the more for being a Jew. He, too, wanted things both ways. He wished for the social connections of a Prussian nobleman, but also guarded the financial connections of a Jewish banker. It was not, after all, as if his Jewishness had not been greatly useful. His position depended, in good part, on the whole Jewish network of friendships and long-standing relations that played so great a role in national and international finance. He was at the peak of a very powerful and exposed special group in German society.

Another aspect of Bleichröder's position also needs to be mentioned. The financial power of Berlin went hand in hand with the forcible establishment of Prussian hegemony over the Reich. Both accompanied the rapid modernization of German society. Not surprisingly, those who found Prussian domination galling and economic modernization uncongenial were inclined to attack Bleichröder as the most vulnerable aspect of Bismarck's juggernaut. That many of the disaffected were also Catholics, whom Bismarck had legally persecuted for their faith, no doubt gave them further cause for grievance. Bleichröder – Bismarck's ally and creature, Berlin's biggest banker, and a Jew – must have seemed a very tempting target.

In any event, by the 1880s, Bleichröder's exposure became increasingly painful. Anti-Semitic propaganda grew more vehement and vicious, and the attacks against him personally cast a dark shadow over his later years. He was hurt and embarrassed to be singled out and was always hoping his powerful friends would rush to his public defense. Occasionally they did, but often they did not. Crude populist anti-Semitism was never very good form among the upper classes. It is interesting, for example, that Bismarck's notorious dislike of Wagner stemmed in good part from distaste for Wagner's vulgar anti-Semitism. But the Bismarckian political elites were a tough breed, used to that particular rhetorical violence that was part of Bismarck's legacy to the German political tradition. No doubt, Bismarck felt Bleichröder could take care of himself.

There were, however, more fundamental and sinister reasons why conservatives were reluctant to confront populist anti-Semitism head-on. Increasingly, all political forces were finding it necessary to mobilize a mass base. The way was set by the Social Democrats who, despite official disfavor, were becoming a highly efficient mass party. Other political forces were constrained to transform themselves from parliamentary cabals into mass organizations. German party politics, like German industry, was becoming an affair of giant integrated firms and cartels. Conservatives found their natural base in the still substantial agrarian population, organized in 1892 into an Agrarian League. They also hoped to attract the lower-middle-class vote – small tradesmen, traditional craftsmen, and minor officials who resented the general evolution toward a mass industrial society and were often ill-equipped to maintain their dignity within it.

To appeal to a broad mass audience, a traditional party needed a popular ideology to rival Marxism. Whereas the

National Liberals often turned to imperialism, conservatives turned to an antiindustrial agrarianism, given intellectual form by a group of academic economists, most prominently Adolf Wagner, Karl Oldenberg, and Max Sering. Together, these economists formulated and legitimized a complex rationale for conservative agrarian interests. Modern societies, they argued, would have to choose between two organizing socioeconomic models *Agrarstaat* and *Industriestaat*. Each of the competing models provided a holistic organization of society and government, but derived from contrary principles. The agrarian state, as they saw it, based itself upon the corporate virtues of duty, hierarchy, sacrifice, and justice, whereas the industrial state was based on pleasure, ambition, and egoism. The agrarian state typified the best of Germany's Prussian heritage, whereas industrial capitalism was a British creation, founded on the principles of Manchester Liberalism. This Liberalism they found essentially immoral. Under it, economic and social life were left to the mercy of a market mechanism, driven by asocial, egoistic selfishness. In the fragmented and uncaring industrial society that resulted, patriarchal leadership gave way to remote manipulation through the stock exchange. Aristocracy was replaced by a plutocracy of grasping millionaires. Labor was dehumanized and became merely another commodity.

Parallels between conservative and Marxist critiques of capitalism were obvious. Both believed industrial society inherently unstable, and for many of the same reasons. Only if Germany returned to an agrarian society, these conservative theorists argued, could it avoid the domestic revolution that the Marxists awaited. Not only did these conservative economists appropriate Marx's domestic analysis (as Marx himself had borrowed from English conservatives before him), they also anticipated Lenin's international analysis. Simultaneous industrialization in all Western countries would make international conflict inevitable, they argued. All Western states, with their rapidly growing populations, were seeking economic equilibrium through industrialization and the export of manufactures. All were emphasizing industry and sacrificing agriculture; hence, all were growing more and more dependent upon foreign trade. Inevitably, industrial states would struggle ever more viciously for foreign markets and food. In the unavoidable conflict, Germany would prove exceptionally ill-favored, particularly against Britain, which possessed an island base, a great fleet, and a vast sheltered colonial system. In short, sacrificing agriculture was not only debauching Germany's best cultural traditions and leading to an ignoble, unstable domestic society, it was also gravely jeopardizing national survival in an increasingly competitive international arena.

Such a coherent and comprehensive body of antimodernist ideas, legitimized by a distinguished band of agrarian economists and widely circulated in agrarian circles, helped transform the conservative party, traditional spokesman of the Junker agrarians, into a mass party with a national ideology. How seriously conservative political leaders took this antimodernist ideology may be questioned. In the end, their main electoral alliance was, after all, with heavy industry. Bismarck himself was perhaps typical of their mentality. He, too, doubtless wanted things all ways. He wanted modernization, or saw it as inevitable, and few leaders did more to bring it about. But like any sensitive conservative, or liberal for that matter, he detested many modernist values and feared their consequences. He thus wanted a Germany that was both powerful and modern but in which the traditional elites and values might hold their place. A mass conservative party would at least preserve something of the power and values of the traditional elites, and hence restrain the headlong pace of change.

Unfortunately, however, the way conservatives chose to build their political base led them into a Faustian compromise with the demonic forces they feared, a compromise unworthy of their values and fatal to their interests. For the antimodernist ideology was not only anti-British, but anti-Semitic. Our economists, to be sure, avoided crude anti-Semitism. But even they saw the Jews as particularly virulent carriers of the egotistical spirit of industrial capitalism. Less fastidious agrarians turned to anti-Semitic rabble-rousing. And for those who needed a dash of pseudo-scientific modernity with their conservatism, Gobineau's racist doctrines, imported and marketed by Wagner, were always at hand. But however rationalized, anti-Semitism, plausibly linked as it was with their whole antimodernist ideology, was a political tool not easily dispensed with by conservative elites searching for a mass base. Rich Jews like Bleichröder were all-too-convenient symbols for those disaffected with change. The conservatives, of course, were playing a game as dangerous as it was ignoble. For by legitimizing and exacerbating anti-Semitism, they were encouraging populist forces opposed not only to Jews, but to the whole imperial establishment.

It is interesting to see the aged Bleichröder, tormented by the growing virulence of the anti-Semitic press, making this very point to William I. Bleichröder was particularly incensed to find a court chaplain, Stöcker, increasingly prominent among anti-Semitic agitators. Bleichröder pleaded for his sovereign's ". . . High patriarchial protection for myself, but not only for myself, rather for a whole class of loyal subjects of Your Majesty, who surely are not useless subjects of the state."[6] Stöcker, Bleichröder argued, was turning "the bitter struggle against the Jews [into] a social struggle against property as such." "My name . . . is invoked not only as a target for persecution but is branded as the prototype of all capital, of the stock market, of all prosperity, and of all evil."[7] This anti-Semi-

---

[6] Fritz Stern, *Gold and Iron. Bismarck, Bleichroder and the Building of the German Empire* (New York: Knopf, 1977), p. 513.

[7] Ibid., p. 513.

tic agitation, countenanced by conservative Christian circles, was worse than Social Democracy, Bleichröder argued. The masses were being stirred to their depths, and would unleash "a terrible social revolution which would threaten all society."[8] That revolution was being powerfully assisted, moreover, by embittered middle-class Jews who were being driven from their traditional conservative loyalties.

As we know, but William did not, subsequent events would prove Bleichröder tragically prescient. To be fair, no one could easily imagine the Nazi crimes in Imperial Germany. Even the conservatives' use of anti-Semites was never unqualified and varied with political circumstances. Rhetorical violence was, after all, a common feature of imperial politics. Despite the abuse, moreover, Bleichröder remained rich, powerful, and protected. In this respect, Jews fared better than Catholics, who had been subjected to active legal persecution. An exhausting war, humiliating peace, ruinous inflation, and desperate depression occurred before a political movement actively devoted to anti-Semitism came to power. But the path was smoothed by the agrarian conservatives, desperately menaced in the late 1920s by agricultural depression. They hoped, by sponsoring the Nazis, to dominate a reformed Reich. When the Nazis came to power, the conservative elites soon lost control of the forces they had legitimized. As Dahrendorf argues convincingly, and as Bleichröder foretold, no one did more to destroy traditional German society than Hitler. Probably no one hated the old elites more.

Rauschning's *The Revolution of Nihilism*, written in the winter of 1937–8, is perhaps the classic statement of the conservative awakening. This Baltic patrician had seen in Hitler's demogogic talents the instrument for restoring and rejuvenating the traditional order. But Hitler's demonic energy would never recreate either the rational order or the

8 Ibid., p. 514.

settled privileges of a traditional society. Hitler embodied the very antithesis of such a society. What Rauschning learned early, the aristocratic army discovered later. The officers' plot of 1944 was the culmination of this awakening. The flower of Prussian Junkerdom perished at the hands of the Gestapo.

The whole story of Germany's traditional elites and anti-Semitism might be seen as yet another episode in the modern Faustian drama. It illustrates not so much atavistic reversion to ancestral racism as an abiding preoccupation with power. One is tempted to say it shows more the influence of Machiavelli than Wagner. But as so often happens when old morality is sold for new power, those elites who should have known better are generally prominent among the victims. The Germans, however, are unlikely to be the last to experience this lesson.

How, finally, does this discussion of anti-Semitism contribute to our study of the German Problem? For a start, the phenomenon of "anti-Semitism" needs a more sensitive and precise analysis than it often receives. For our purposes at least three distinct categories can be delineated. There is first what might be called "objective" anti-Semitism. The Bismarckian Jews were a powerful, cohesive, and visible minority. Many of their most prominent members were closely allied in the popular mind with the forcible domination of Prussia over Germany and with what that hegemony brought in its train: rapid economic modernization along uncongenial lines and eclipse and even persecution for those life styles, provincial attachments, and cultural and religious values that resisted. Also "objective" was the reaction of older elites to the ostentatious vulgarity and social climbing of new wealth. Even if we sympathize with the nouveaux riches, we cannot reasonably deny the more established German classes the right to prefer their own values and resent their displacement.

The second category may be called "social" anti-Semitism. It is the typical snobbery of upper and especially middle classes toward the rising Jew. It differs from "objective" anti-Semitism in that it is an unreasoning automatic reaction to stereotypes rather than individuals. To have disliked Bleichröder as a tedious, comic, or sinister upstart may have been quite objective. To have disliked all Jews automatically as little Bleichröders was not. Obviously, many people who have the first reaction often find themselves sliding into the second. The capacity and predisposition to generalize is, after all, thought to be the fundamental characteristic that separates human from animal intelligence. It is a mixed blessing. Societies and individuals have to teach themselves over and over to guard against generalizations that distort the warm real world of particulars. Anti-Semitism is but one of the multitudinous misuses of abstraction by which societies impoverish and embitter themselves. But this "social" anti-Semitism was no worse in Imperial Germany than elsewhere in Europe. And certainly it did not prevent Jews from reaching high economic, social, and even political positions in Germany and Austria as the prominence of Jews in Imperial Berlin and Vienna gives ample witness.

Ugly as this "social" anti-Semitism may have been, it was very different from a third category — "political" anti-Semitism. This may be described as the deliberate use of the stereotyped Jew as a hateful symbol to stimulate popular discontent within the society either to attack the establishment or perhaps to deflect attacks away from it. It is this politicized and manipulative populist anti-Semitism that Germany began to experience in the 1870's, and that reached a certain peak in the 1880s, when Conservatives flirted with coopting it, and, of course, reached its lunatic apogee with the Nazis.

What is the point of these categories? Even in this painful and treacherous sphere, the aggressive criminality of the Nazi era cannot plausibly be laid to some autonomous evolution of Germany's inner cultural shortcomings. Anti-Semitism did not grow steadily, from Bismarck to Hitler, until it came to dominate German political life. For our varieties of anti-Semitism are not interchangeable; nothing requires one to follow from the other. It may be possible to dislike some Jews intensely, and for good reasons, without disliking all Jews in general. And prejudice against Jews in general need not be politicized – let alone turned into the principal focus of a political mass movement.

Anti-Semitism of this third kind did, of course, exist in Germany from imperial times. And it did achieve a certain respectability because of its affinity with the anticapitalist ideology of the Conservatives. But is was not a dominant force among even the Conservatives, let alone among the other political groupings. Hitler, to be sure, made it the centerpiece of his own antimodernist ideology. But it seems doubtful that anti-Semitism was what gave his brew its principal appeal among Germans as a whole. In any event, not until war, humiliation, and repeated economic disaster broke down the normal structures of the German state was the way open to an adventurer like Hitler. Those Conservatives who saw in Hitler a popular force to be manipulated, and who helped him to power, were habituated to this particularly vile form of rabble-rousing. Anti-Semitism lay within their bag of political tricks. But it was hardly their driving passion. That passion was self-preservation and power. In a world that had lost its moorings, they were prepared to make a pact with the Devil himself. In doing so, not only did they dishonor themselves and their class, but the Germany Bismarck had created was destroyed.

*The German Idealist Tradition and
its Political Consequences*

Since the war, a distinguished school of historians and sociologists has sought the key to the German Problem in the prevalence of a strong Idealist tradition in German philosophy. According, for example, to the distinguished contemporary German historian, Karl Dietrich Bracher:

Neither the history nor the decline of political science in Germany are [sic] understandable unless account is taken of the influence of the old-established doctrine of the state and its confrontation with western [sic] tradition. . . . The relationship between the concept of the state and democracy undoubtedly holds one of the keys to any understanding of this distinctive German development – both in German politics and in German political science. It is significant that applications of this question to British, American or even French conditions produces no comparably illuminating answer. There the state has never been regarded as a sovereign entity over and above social and political groupings; alternatively the idea went into limbo as a result of successful revolution.[9]

Bracher goes on to argue that this German "concept of the state was nonpolitical . . . the notion that the state was something above party, in so far as it was not mere ideological camouflage, betrayed an unpolitical misconception of the nature and function of the state."[10]

In the same vein, the well-known contemporary German sociologist, Ralf Dahrendorf, finds that this "Hegelian notion of the state has influenced political thought and practical politics in Germany to the present day. By way of Lassalle it slipped . . . into the baggage of the labor movement."[11] Dahrendorf finds in this Hegelian tradition the explanation or at least the expression of an unfortunate "German propensity for synthesis" a propensity that means "that all institutions of German society are characterized by the attempt to evade conflict or to abolish it in superior authorities and institutions. . . . What the consequences of such an approach are, German history of the last hundred years had demonstrated."[12]

[9] Karl Dietrich Bracher, *The German Dilemma: The Throes of Political Emancipation* (London: Weidenfeld and Nicolson, 1974), pp. 5–6.

[10] Ibid., p. 9.

[11] Ralf Dahrendorf, *Society and Democracy in Germany* (New York: Doubleday, Anchor, 1969), p. 192.

[12] Ibid.

At first look, such views would seem difficult to contest, particularly when presented by two such knowledgeable analysts of German politics, men whose moral sincerity and goodwill are clear on every page of their writing. It seems difficult, moreover, to argue that the history of the German state reveals an excess of democracy or a deficiency of authoritarianism. Nevertheless, this whole approach, although laudable in its aims and doubtless beneficial in its effects, suffers from a fundamental flaw: Its reaction to the Idealist tradition is excessive and, as a consequence, its diagnosis of German political culture is seriously distorted. Indeed, one of the most harmful aftereffects of Germany's wars has been the suppression of the Idealist political tradition on the grounds that it is "German." In my view, that tradition still offers the best framework for understanding the modern condition.

In effect, both Bracher and Dahrendorf postulate a "Liberal" or "Anglo-Saxon" theory of the state, and contrast it favorably with the Idealist, Hegelian, or "German" conception. How meaningful is this distinction, and what does it contribute to understanding the German Problem?

Even a summary answer requires a rather lengthy excursion into political philosophy. Behind the two notions of the state, Idealist and Liberal, lie two contrasting approaches to defining liberty. In the terminology popularized by Sir Isaiah Berlin's celebrated essay, the Idealist tradition emphasizes a "positive" conception of liberty whereas the Liberal tradition's emphasis is "negative." What is the broad character of these two approaches, and how does it shape their view of the state?

The Idealist tradition is "positive" in its notions of liberty because it emphasizes the social and economic preconditions for liberty. Freedom, by which is meant self-development, is seen to require a favorable setting, a Good Society. To be free, the individual must live in a "state," that is to say a rationally organized community that provides the needed framework to develop his freedom. The state in this sense is the ideal, the political community as it ought to be to fulfill human potential, not necessarily the political community as it may actually exist. Hence, the "idea" of the state is the norm, or the potential, against which may be measured the concrete arrangements of a society at any historical moment. Behind these notions of the state and freedom lies a fundamental belief in some ideal form, some proper pattern for development both for the individual and for the society. The Idealist philosopher sees the definition and pursuit of this ideal form as the main business of life both for individuals and for the community as a whole. Individuals and societies succeed in life insofar as they achieve some functional version of the human ideal. How the supposedly universal elements of this human ideal may be reconciled with changing particular circumstances has been, from the days of Plato and Aristotle, the classic problem in this tradition. Modern Idealists, following Hegel, have preoccupied themselves with finding in history the key to how human and social ideals have "developed" to shape society in an increasingly rational form. In summary, freedom in this Idealist perspective is not merely the absence of direct coercion, but also the achievement of a certain level of individual and communal development within the possibilities of a particular historical context.

The negative or "Liberal" tradition, by contrast, takes a far more restricted definition of freedom. Liberty is simply the absence of outside interference. In the abstract, the more the state interferes with the free-agency of the individual, the less liberty remains to him. The more laws, the less liberty. Behind this view of liberty lies a different view of the individual. Whereas the Idealist is concerned with how the individual can develop himself, the Liberal tends to view the individual as already formed. Man's problem is less to develop than to protect what he already has. The whole tradition, therefore, focuses not on how the community can help individual development, but rather on how the state can so easily oppress it. A major problem for this tradition lies in finding some way to check government without denying it an adequate basis for legitimacy. Liberal writers have traditionally employed the concept of a "social contract." Authority is legitimate when free men, out of rational self-interest, agree to set up a civil state. As a practical matter, some liberty must be sacrificed to a government in order to enjoy the rest. The question always remains who decides how much liberty is given up and how much remains? Hobbes's classical analysis reached an unpalatable conclusion that has haunted the Liberal tradition ever after. Because the "natural" state of mankind is "the war of all against all," he decided, maintaining order required a sovereign power that was absolute. Locke, the other classic figure of this Liberal tradition, avoided Hobbes's conclusion by reversing its premise. For Locke, harmony rather than war was the normal state of affairs, except where unnatural monopolies of political power, like monarchies or privileged aristocracies, provided the opportunity for exploitation. Thus, Locke concluded, ultimate sovereignty could safely be vested in a majority of the "people." Locke's Liberal political ideal, in short, was a political version of the laissez-aller of the free market.

Bracher and, in particular, Dahrendorf take this broad distinction between Idealist and Liberal conceptions of freedom and project it into two contrasting models of political behavior. In their view, German Idealism, by stressing the moral identity between the purposes of individuals and the community, has dangerously heightened the German state's prestige. Moreover, the underlying Idealist notion of some "best" solution to conflicts, to be discovered by the exercise of trained reason, encourages citizens to be "apolitical" – meekly submissive to authoritarian technocracy. By contrast, in societies that fit the Liberal model, the state has had none of this overblown prestige, they say. Instead of expecting public experts to find ideal solutions, citizens and groups vigorously assert their own interests in competition with each other in the political marketplace. In these healthier societies, Dahrendorf argues, the notion of a common good to be sustained by the state is restricted to certain "rules of the game" that exist to limit the mayhem that one interest group may practice on another. Liberal politics in such a society is like sport. Rival teams compete vigorously within a frame of formal rules and general sportsmanship.

The general conclusion of this sort of analysis is more or less self-evident: Germany has had a strong predilection toward authoritarian and totalitarian government, in part at least because German political culture reflects the Idealist rather than the Liberal notion of freedom. Thanks to their Idealism, Germans are essentially "apolitical" submissive to technocratic authority, impatient of conflict and competition, and inclined to endow their states with excessive moral prestige. For opposite reasons, the British and Americans are healthy libertarians. What is the matter with this view?

It may be questioned on three rather decisive grounds: First, philosophically, the whole distinction between positive and negative freedom is simpleminded, as is the critique of Idealism in general. Second, historically, it is not self-evident that one tradition should be called German and the other British. Finally, the derivative models of Liberal versus Idealist societies have little to do with the workings of either German or British societies.

To start with the philosophical point: The limitations of the Liberal critique of Idealism flow from the limitations of the Liberal notion of freedom itself. The Liberal view is not so much wrong as incomplete, the consequence of its inadequate view of freedom. Obviously, no society can be called free that does not permit the individual an assured sphere of private liberty with reasonable scope for personal action. Modern Idealist thought, in fact, has used this necessity for elbowroom as the justification for private property. To be free, an individual must have a certain sphere within which, broadly speaking, he can do as he pleases. But if such negative rights that protect citizens from interference are essential for liberty, they are not sufficient in themselves to achieve it. Property rights are not worth much in a society that has fallen into chaos or where a large part of the population is ignorant, unhealthy, undernourished, and exploited. The Liberal's negative rights, by themselves, cannot constitute an adequate definition of freedom in the extraordinarily complex and vulnerable societies in which modern man lives.

Similarly incomplete is the Liberal societal model, with its enthusiasm for the unfettered clash of private interests in a "free market." Freedom clearly does require an open society where interests are free to articulate their demands. But no democratic society will long survive if egotistical assertions of private interest are not contained by some consensus of common identity and public interest. That consensus must, moreover, serve as the foundation for an active public power able to cope successfully with the many challenges that the modern environment poses to the perpetuation of humane ideals. Again, no society is likely to arrive at an acceptable consensus without the mutual knowledge and understanding that arise from the clash of interest groups. But without an active, creative public mediator, modern society soon resembles the worst expectations of Hobbes' war of all against all. Here once more, the Liberal view is not so much wrong as incomplete.

It is striking how much postwar writing about democratic political and social institutions has ignored these rather commonplace observations of political philosophy. Nowhere more egregiously, of course, than in the postwar writing about Germany. Germans themselves seem determined to reject the richness of their own philosophical tradition in exchange for a rather scanty version of what they take to be the British and American. In this respect they do violence not only to political philosophy but to history as well. For it slanders British philosophical culture to equate it with such an arid Liberal tradition. Were Idealism exclusively German and Liberalism entirely British, Nietzsche's dictum would be fully justified: "They are not a philosophical race – the English. . . ."[13] In fact, Idealism permeates British political thought, and indeed, finds there some of its most distinguished expressions. In modern times, a British Idealist tradition runs from Hooker through Burke and Coleridge, has great influence on various Victorian figures, including John Stuart Mill, Disraeli, and Gladstone, and reaches its most comprehensive philosophical expression in the late-nineteenth- and early-twentieth-century British "neo-Hegelians." These venerable sages – Greene, Bradley, and Bosanquet, to name the most prominent – dominated formal British philosophy until, thanks in part to wartime propaganda against "German" ideas, their influence was gradually supplanted by the logical postivism of Russell, Wittgenstein, Popper, and Ayer. Although no one can deny that British logical positivism springs from an ancient and honorable British nominalism, to suggest that it is Britain's only major tradition is not very good intellectual history. Figures like Greene, Bradley, and Bosanquet seem no less firmly rooted in British culture than the Viennese immigrants who did so much to revive logical postivism.

Should anyone doubt the significance of the Idealist tradition in other European countries, they need only think of Croce in Italy or Bergson in France. Indeed, the political ideas of General de Gaulle reveal his fundamentally Idealist perspective at every turn. The same point may be made

13 Friedrich Nietzsche, *Beyond Good and Evil*, in *The Philosophy of Nietzsche* (New York: Modern Library, 1954), p. 565.

about American political thought. John Dewey, for all his great qualities, was hardly the only American philosopher. A long American Idealist tradition stretches back through the nineteenth century to Puritan and Anglican thought of colonial times. John Kennedy's famous inaugural cry, "Ask not what your country can do for you, but what you can do for your country" suggests how much our contemporary ideas are shaped by the Idealist tradition.

In short, political Idealism is not merely a German specialty, eschewed by more prudent neighbors. Instead, it is part of that general rise of Romanticism that spread throughout the cultural life of the last century and continues into our own. Britain – the country of Burke, Blake, Wordsworth, Coleridge, Shelley, Ruskin, and Disraeli – was hardly innocent of Romanticism or political Idealism.

What is true of British thought is also, in fact, true of British politics. The Liberal model of a contentiousness uncomplicated by collective Idealism certainly does not describe the way Anglo-Saxon societies actually function – today or in the past. No meaningful description of the American or British political systems can ignore, for a start, the moral prestige of the office of president or prime minister – a prestige flowing from the claim that their office embodies, in effect, a "General Will." These "executives" are not merely "umpires" who keep the rules of the political game, but they are the major formulators and advocates of public policy. Their avowed function is to represent the whole public in distinction to the partial interests of industry, agriculture, labor, or even the legislature. Insofar as they appear to fail in this function, they lose their prestige and moral authority. In short, "Anglo-Saxon" politics is not merely a free-for-all of special interests, without any mediating public authority to shape a positive policy. Indeed, insofar as any society begins to approximate such a Liberal model, it becomes increasingly ungovernable. Historical experience suggests that laissez-faire – for that is what the Liberal model seems to be – can prevail only under very special circumstances. Either it reflects the domination of certain interests who use the market as a mechanism for organizing their own political and economic hegemony, or it corresponds with a period of exceptional abundance, when rising expectations have not yet caught up with expanding resources.

Ironically, whereas the Liberal model fails to describe the societies that are supposed to have inspired it, it does in some respects fit Imperial Germany. Germany never lacked groups willing to assert their particular interests with all the vigor a Liberal society is supposed to require. Where, for example, was the "apolitical German" when it came to tariff legislation, social welfare, the fleet, or the army? Bismarck's political strategy, of course, deliberately encouraged all these groups to be as outrageously demanding as possible and, as a consequence, to make himself the only locus for the agglomeration of interests into some kind of rational general policy. Thus, only he, not Parliament, could claim legitimately to embody the general interest. He succeeded all too well. As a result, the initiative for national policy was held by an authoritarian executive – not because there was too little bloody-minded contentiousness in Parliament, but because there was too much. The Reichstag was ineffective not because its deputies were always pursuing the general good to the neglect of particular needs, but because the parties seldom could rise above the vigorous advocacy of selfish interests. Consequently, German Parliaments could never serve as the basis for an effective government, either in Bethmann's era or during the Weimar regime. This, it might be said, was Bismarck's "Liberal" legacy.

Although I cannot claim to have done full justice to the arguments of such sophisticated writers as Bracher and Dahrendorf, I believe I have captured their essential point. How is it that their Liberal critique, so obviously deficient, has enjoyed so prominent a place in postwar writing about Germany?

The explanation can hardly be traced to a lack of intelligence or knowledge. It lies, I expect, in an understandably exaggerated reaction to the horrors of Nazism by a generation that has suffered so deeply from it. For a society convalescing from the trauma and shame of totalitarianism, Liberalism, for all its intellectual shortcomings, has seemed far safer than Idealism, with its positive notions about freedom. Idealism provides a political formula that consciously strives to create consensus around a particular vision. The Ideal, the practical definition of the Good Life, demands to be discovered and articulated. But the results of the search may, of course, be bad as well as good. As both Hitler and Stalin amply illustrated, Idealist rhetoric can be manipulated to serve the most perverted notions of freedom. A society can find unity in plundering neighbors, managing the world, or murdering its Jews. After their Nazi experience, Germans may be forgiven for finding a negative skepticism the safest refuge for liberty.

But despite its good intentions, this neo-Liberal view carries its own dangers. For with its bias against substantive visions, it perpetually seeks as a substitute some political machinery, some structure of habits and procedures that can guarantee a free society regardless of the substantive quality of that society. Obviously, social and political structures are vastly important. But they are not enough to secure a worthy society. Societies cannot safely put off finding collective rational goals any more than individuals can safely avoid seeking some rational meaning and plan for their private lives. The questions of what is a Good Life, and how to live it, cannot simply be pushed aside by "value-free" social science, peddling some magic political mechanism that guarantees freedom without philosophical effort or moral discipline. A divisive selfishness that makes democracy fragile is the natural condition of a society that has no larger common vision. Temporary abundance may temporarily put off the day of reckoning, but the crisis will come sooner or later. It is better to take up the challenge than to pretend it does not exist. For no set of social mechanisms can long flourish in the absence of creative political imagination. The neo-Liberal tradition tries to replace that imagination with its political version of the free market. It is a vain presumption, and one of the advantages of the Idealist tradition is that it knows better. Rather than endlessly repeating ill-informed attacks on the Idealist school, German or English, modern analysts would do better to study it seriously. It is far richer, on the whole, than logical positivism.

Conclusion: The Taming of Power

I began this chapter by renouncing anything so ambitious as a comprehensive theory of German society and culture. My own observations are hardly meant to provide a general theory, but rather to suggest skepticism at conventional theories about German political culture. As the postwar era comes to a close, perhaps those who have formulated these theories should stand back and take a fresh look.

For me, the study of modern German society suggests two broad lessons. Neither is particularly novel. The first is the fragility of all modern societies and the relevance of what may be called the Faust theme in understanding that fragility. The second is the danger of "overloading" the international system.

Every modern society has struggled to discipline an otherwise self-destructive pursuit of power and wealth through some notion of a balanced, legitimate, and good social order – a notion that has to have an international as well as a national dimension. The moral issues involved are hardly new. The struggle between will and reason preoccupies Western thought from the very beginning. Significantly, perhaps, the two most ambitious single works of German creative genius in the nineteenth century, Goethe's *Faust* and Wagner's *Ring*, both chart the struggle between power and natural order.

Whenever a society modernizes very rapidly, the Faustian drive grows intense. Modern technology not only permits hitherto unimaginable control over nature, but, at the same time, radically alters the scale of human affairs. Unstructured urban societies provide great opportunities for manipulating by new techniques of mass communication. And the uneven spread of technology among nations creates unprecedented opportunities for manipulating foreign peoples. Thus, modern power is not only greater in intensity and scale, but more able to insulate itself from the direct human relationships that can condition even the most abject formal domination.

The worship of Goethe notwithstanding, the insights of German art have not served to prevent the catastrophes of German politics. But, once again, those catastrophes cannot credibly be seen as the outcome of some autonomous evolution of the inherent weakness of German culture. Weaknesses there surely were, in Germany as everywhere else. But the breakdown was far more plausibly the consequence of the intense pressure brought to bear on the society from its external problems. That pressure seems less Germany's particular fault than the inevitable consequence of the breakdown of measure in the system as a whole. The imperialism that led to the First World War was itself the consequence of expanding demands confronted by shrinking resources, a combination that overloaded the international system beyond the possibilities of peaceful adjustment. Germany, the late arrival, became the major focus of tension. Doubtless German diplomacy was rather inept, particularly in the Bülow era. But the best diplomacy in the world was unlikely to avoid a German confrontation with the older powers. For the more established nations had a thrust to power no less vigorous than Germany's. All European countries were afflicted with an increasing tension between boundless aspirations and rational order. In such a world, the Germans proved exceptionally vulnerable. As the late arrival, Germany was, by definition, the "aggressor." No doubt the German middle classes had become more narrowly national after Bismarck than their British and French counterparts, who had had time to grow more relaxed and secure with their national power. But the Germans, given their experience before unification, could hardly be blamed for wanting a national state to match their aggressive neighbors, nor for being worried that these neighbors would not accept it. And if the Germans seemed paranoically concerned with force, they were, in fact, open on all sides to their most powerful military enemies, as well as peculiarly vulnerable to a naval blockade. As the First World War rather amply demonstrated, German military fears may have been self-fulfilling, but certainly were not without foundation.

Once the Great War began, the military struggle gradually grew hopeless; the strain broke down the German state and opened the way to the rule of adventurers. Throughout the Weimar era, the state never recovered its stability. Indeed, with inflation and depression, the wartime pressure grew even greater. Finally, the German state went berserk under Hitler.

To repeat an earlier conclusion, it is hard to escape from the rather traditional Leninist view that Imperial Germany's international problem sprang less from its peculiar domestic characteristics than from the timing of its development. The lesson is not that Germans are peculiarly wicked, but rather that even a deeply rooted civilization can rapidly descend into barbarism – at home and abroad – if put under intense sustained pressure. No doubt, it is good for the Germans to study their past and renew their shame. For the rest of us, the study of Germany's horrors should induce humility rather than smugness. There, but for the grace of God, might have gone any of us. And indeed, if we are not careful, there lies the future as well as the past.

7

The German Problem after 1945

Old Options and the Postwar System

What has happened to the German Problem since 1945? For both Germans and their neighbors, many of the traditional problems have seemed resolved. Abroad, no neighbors have been menaced by German aggression. At home, each part of Germany has undergone a political mutation. The German Federal Republic has become steadfastly liberal, the German Democratic Republic militantly communist. Neither postwar German remnant has faced the Reich's problem of isolation – its incapacity to fit within a regional or world political-economic order. Instead, both postwar German states have been integrated into the bipolar world of superpower systems. Indeed, both states are the creations of that bipolar system. How much continuity is there, then, between the German Problem of the past and the German situation since 1945?

One difference is obvious. Today, instead of one German state, as in Hitler's time, there are two – three with Austria. This forced separation has seemed so drastic and untenable that, for many analysts, Germany's principal problem has

161

become its reunification. No solution, however, has seemed plausible. For no matter how unnatural it may have appeared initially, Germany's dismemberment was the logical outcome of partitioning Europe into Eastern and Western spheres. The Cold War between the superpowers quickly froze the temporary military demarcations into rigid political-economic boundaries. And Germany's neighbors blessed its division. Indeed, although partition was clearly imposed upon them, the Germans themselves were not altogether unwilling collaborators, even at the outset. In the West, Adenauer's regime established a liberal capitalist welfare state according to the ideals of his Christian Democratic Party. In the East, Ulbricht's communist elite, under more trying circumstances, built its favored version of a disciplined socialist utopia. Just as Bismarck is said to have limited his ambition to a smaller Reich, in order to preserve its cohesion through Prussian dominance, so Adenauer and Ulbricht might be said to have preferred their smaller, more cohesive and, by their respective lights, more attractive states to a united nation. In effect, after Hitler's catastrophe, the older German pattern of *cuius regio, eius religio* was found to have its compensations.

In any event, the opportunity for reunification probably never really existed. Neither superpower could have been expected to abandon its part of Germany to the other. And despite considerable tergiversation in the early postwar years, neither, having just barely defeated Hitler, was really eager for a reunited neutral Germany, with all its potential, ideologically and militarily disengaged. Moreover, without the contribution of its Germany, neither superpower could probably have built a stable system out of its portion of Europe. And the Germans themselves, at least in the West, soon grew attached to the comforts of integration within a larger and relatively stable systemic order. In short, a united neutralist Germany, with all its uncertainties, had little practical appeal either for Germany's conquerors or among the Germans themselves.

With postwar Germany firmly divided, is the traditional German Problem therefore solved? The question seems most relevant for the Federal Republic, the major fragment of the old Germany and still a major power in the world. In some respects, despite its heavy political liabilities, Germany under the Federal Republic has managed to find a more comfortable place in the international order than under either imperial or Nazi regimes. Above all, the Federal Republic has succeeded in the economic sphere. Initially, West Germany's economy was directly controlled by the Allies. One current in early American thinking was embodied in the so-called Morgenthau Plan. Outright revenge combined with fears of overproduction to envisage dismantling German industry altogether. But more temperate views prevailed and German recovery was deemed essential, a determination strengthened as Western European recovery stalled and the Cold War grew intense. West Germany was given full place within the Marshall Plan. Moreover, the Allied currency reform of 1948, sustained by a policy of tight money and balanced budgets, endowed Germany with a stable and undervalued currency, a firm foundation for export promotion and domestic investment. Political reconstruction proceeded along with economic. In 1949, the Allies formally established the Federal Republic and gradually lifted the remaining economic disabilities. The Korean War prompted the United States to promote and finance a major rearmament of the West, including ultimately the Federal Republic. Substantial flows of direct American aid fueled a major Western boom. Of all the European countries, Germany proved the best situated to profit. Hence, Germany's "miracle" of the 1950s.

A variety of factors favored Germany. Europe's industrial reconstruction provided great opportunities for the traditional German capital-goods industry, opportunities that were exploited with customary efficiency despite efforts to prevent the old cartels. Banks continued to play a major role in promoting and rationalizing industrial development. Wages were relatively low, savings and corporate profits high, and resources efficiently channeled into industrial investment. An enlightened blend of economic, social, labor, and managerial policies produced an exceptionally stable version of welfare capitalism. Ironically, the postwar Germans not only profited from their imperial heritage of an export-oriented capital-goods industry, but also from the Nazi preoccupation with an autarchic industrial structure. As a consequence, postwar Germany was now easily oriented toward exporting, but had less need for industrial imports than its Western competitors. And although losing the East deprived West Germany of its major native source of food and raw materials, the United States' postwar system was making primary products abundant and cheap on world markets. Costly German agriculture conveniently disappeared just as the terms of trade were turning steadily in favor of manufactures. Losing the East also favored West Germany's labor market. Throughout the fifties, a steady stream of highly competent, motivated, and assimilable refugee labor flowed westward. Thus augmented, the West German labor supply was abundant, disciplined, and relatively cheap. Low wages, combined with conservative monetary policies and balanced budgets, discouraged inflation and helped keep German export prices highly competitive.

In effect, the "miracle" of the fifties shaped the postwar West German economy in the pre-1914 mold. Germany became an export machine oriented toward heavy industry. The principal difference lay in the disappearance of high-cost East Elbian agriculture. Thus, today's Federal Republic constitutes a rather extreme version of the traditional Little German or world option, with no hope of achieving anything like self-sufficiency in raw materials or markets. In the traditional analysis, such a Germany was supposed to be dangerously vulnerable – likely, in times of stress, to find itself denied raw materials and markets. Those with imperial power were expected to use it whenever Germany's commercial rivalry began to threaten their well-being. That was, after all, how many Germans interpreted the First World War.

Why have none of these difficulties afflicted the Federal Republic? A broad answer springs to mind. West Germany, unlike either the Second or Third Reich, has been securely integrated into a worldwide political-economic system. The American world system has given Germany what the British did not, an accepted and secure place within the international order. Thanks to the United States, West Germany has enjoyed not only military protection against Russia, but secure access to the world's raw materials and markets. America's price, moreover, has not seemed excessive. Since the early postwar days, the Federal Republic has not suffered great interference in its internal government. Certainly no widespread popular disaffection undermines the regime. And West Germans enjoy a standard of living among the highest in the world.

Why has the American price been so low? Some credit must certainly go to American statesmanship. The United States' European hegemony has been intelligent, benevolent, and confident. Enlightenment, to be sure, has been encouraged by the extraordinarily long postwar boom. Nearly every country has been able to enjoy unprecedented growth, hence competition within an open system has remained friendly. Ironically, only Britain has failed to join the general prosperity.

Germany's postwar well-being, moreover, has not based itself solely upon the United States' world system. For within that system, yet potentially separate, has also grown up the European Economic Community (EEC). The states of Europe have allowed their economies to become highly interdependent. An intricate political structure has sought to manage that interdependence and assert Europe's common interests in the world. The consequent confederal Pan-European economy has given Europe a home market with sufficient scale to foster industries competitive with the Americans. Community policies, moreover, have tried to guarantee Europe's essential supplies. A Common Agricultural Policy has moved Europe toward self-sufficiency in food. An Association Policy has reached out to secure Mediterranean, Middle Eastern, and African raw materials and markets. In effect, this continental coalition embodies a contemporary version of Pan-Europe, built around a Franco-German liaison. It offers Germany many of the objectives of the traditional continental option.

From this perspective it is interesting to recall how the Common Market initially provoked considerable conflict among the Federal Republic's political forces. Their struggle had many aspects of the old *continental* versus *world* controversy. Not only did the opposition Social Democrats oppose the nascent European Community, but so did a major element within the Christian Democratic Party itself. In 1957, the issue pitted against each other the two dominant Christian Democrats of the postwar recovery – Konrad Adenauer, the chancellor, and Ludwig Erhard, the economics minister. Both, of course, were staunch partisans of the Atlantic tie with the United States. But within the context of that Atlantic connection, Adenauer favored the EEC and placed great stock in the Franco-German rapprochement as its political core. Erhard, by contrast, was a partisan of the loose European Free Trade Area (EFTA) promoted by the British. Erhard was backed by significant portions of organized industry and commerce, and well as the big labor unions. As a liberal Protestant, he was unenthusiastic about special political ties with France, with its *dirigiste* and Catholic traditions. He preferred Germany to have a direct special relationship with Britain and the United States, without special ties among the Europeans intervening. He was also worried about constraining

German industry within a continental dimension. At heart, Erhard was both more internationalist and more strictly national – the usual Little German pattern. Adenauer, by contrast, although solicitous to preserve the Atlantic tie, especially for its military security, pressed as well for a closely integrated European system built around France and Germany. A Rhineland Catholic, Adenauer was more genuinely European – less "outward looking" beyond Europe, but also less particularly German within it. His policy was, in effect, a new version of *Mitteleuropa*.

Adenauer seemed to prevail. Germany spurned EFTA and went with France into the EEC. Any conflict inherent between Adenauer's Atlantic and European loyalties was diffused by the Americans themselves, who, bemused as they were by the vision of a federal Europe, backed Adenauer over his more Atlanticist rival. Perhaps as a result of so fundamental a quarrel, Adenauer refused to resign, as previously arranged, to let Erhard become chancellor. Their struggle continued through the early sixties, with Adenauer pursuing further Franco-German arrangements with de Gaulle, a partnership that Erhard and his friends did their best to stymie. This time their efforts were assisted by the Americans, by then disenchanted generally by the prospect of a more independent Europe and particularly by Adenauer. Finally, in 1963 a confused conjuncture of domestic quarrels, American opposition, and old age combined to force Adenauer out. Erhard succeeded him. Relations with France declined precipitously. By 1966, Erhard himself was maneuvered out of office by the Great Coalition, engineered in large part by the Christian Democrats' "Gaullist" wing – partisans of Europe in general and of the French connection in particular.

The story suggests not only the continuing relevance of the traditional options for German policy, but also the reluctance of the postwar West German state to embrace one at the expense of the other. Thus the Federal Republic has remained an export machine within a worldwide political-economic system, built and still sustained by American economic and military power. At the same time, West Germany forms part of a closely interdependent European system, which offers the scale to compete with the United States, and perhaps the potential for an alternative system should the American empire disintegrate. West German foreign policy has maneuvered to avoid any definitive choice between these novel versions of the traditional options. What is commonly described as Germany's reluctance to choose between the United States and France is also, in effect, Germany's unwillingness to choose between the two traditional strategies for resolving its historic problems. Nothing short of the disintegration of the American liberal imperium or of the European Common Market is likely to force the Germans into a more resolute choice. Understandably, West Germany would much prefer enjoying both options indefinitely.

To be sure, West Germany's advantages have their costs. Incorporation of the Federal Republic into the West is matched by integration of the Democratic Republic into the East; hence the country's division is consolidated. Coming to terms with East Germany has, perforce, been a major preoccupation of the Federal Republic's foreign policy. In effect, the Federal Republic has sought to pursue simultaneously its integration into Atlantic and European systems — itself a complex task — while guarding the possibility of reunification. Even a Bismarck would have great trouble reconciling these three goals. West German statecraft has pursued each, but only far enough not to foreclose the others. In effect, Germany's foreign policy, like Britain's, has been preoccupied with "three circles."

The third circle or line of policy is more than just reunification and is more difficult to define than either European or Atlantic attachments. It is perhaps best described as the "national" option. Its primary concern is doubtless an ultimate reunification with the East, but there are other, more intangible dimensions. The term "national" should not be misunderstood. The supposedly "federal" options of continental and Atlantic integration are also "national," and properly so. They do, however, seek German security and fulfillment through intensified and structured cooperation within a particular group or system of states. By contrast, what is called here the national option involves a more solitary and adventurous exploration of the Federal Republic's diplomatic opportunities. It implies a more conditional and manipulative attitude toward European and Atlantic relations. It means, for example, a greater interest in treating separately with the Russians and Eastern Europeans, without leaving the initiatives to the United States, as spokesman for the "West," or waiting for the cumbersome machinery of "Europe" to formulate and conduct a common policy. It also means more energetic initiatives to explore commercial and political opportunities in the Third World. In short, it means acting like the other Great Powers.

Within limits, the tensions are manageable between national policies to enhance sovereignty and federal policies to intensify interdependence. Indeed the policies may often be complementary. As de Gaulle frequently observed: States make alliances to preserve their sovereignty, not to give it up. In practical terms, the same point holds for international engagements generally, including confederations. Sovereignty in a practical sense means control over the environment in which the nation must live. Like the other Western states, West Germany participates in European and Atlantic structures to enhance real control over its own international and domestic environment. In this sense, federalist policies remain profoundly national. Similarly, national policies may effectively complement federal policies. A strong state can participate more confidently in a confederation than a weak one. Moreover, no national state – least of all one with the experience of modern Germany – can afford to forget the fragility of all inter-state arrangements.

These points are made at some length because they are so frequently forgotten. In the real world, federalist coop-eration is not a renunciation of national self-determination but a technique for its enhancement. Along with the obvious tension between national and federal policies is a less obvious but more significant complementarity. Thus, Federal Germany's national option is not necessarily some sinister and hidden side of its foreign policy, but a natural aspect of the foreign policy of any independent Great Power.

Bonn and the East

The national aspect of German foreign policy inevitably, if not exclusively, concerns itself with reunification, hence with relations between the Federal Republic and its Eastern counterpart, the German Democratic Republic (GDR). Some obvious similarities exist between the position of East Germany in the Soviet system and West Germany in the Western. In both cases, the presiding superpower imposed a regime, but with the cooperation of a German elite that built a society congenial to its ideals. Like its Western counterpart, East Germany has become an export machine. Its participation in an imperial political-eco-nomic system has also given the GDR military security and access to raw materials and markets. To be sure, the Rus-sian economic and political price has been higher than the American. Nevertheless, East Germany has done well enough in recovering its own historic economic standards, and very well in comparison with its Eastern neighbors. Only by contrast with its Western counterpart, and other Western European states, has the GDR's economic position seemed unenviable. Hence the Wall, the repression, the Russian troops, and the inherent limits on the progress of detente in Europe. But with its present panoply of controls apparently assured, East Germany seems a stable if unattractive state. Marxism perhaps furnishes its elites with moral consolations and sanguine long-range expectations. The impressive economic progress, despite all obstacles, feeds expectations of less embarrassing differences in living standards and, in turn, nourishes hopes of a more relaxed relationship with the West. The hopes can easily be exaggerated. Economic parity will not come soon, nor are the vulnerabilities of the Eastern regime limited to the economic sphere. Prospects for "normal" relations are therefore constrained, even if several of the more abrasive and dangerous frictions have been reduced in recent years.

In attempting to square reunification with its Atlantic and European circles, West German policy toward the East has gone through a number of distinct phases. Roughly speaking, throughout the fifties, West German policy under Adenauer was dominated by the prevailing American strategy of "negotiation from strength," essentially a policy of consolidation in the West and immobility toward the East. The Federal Republic refused to recognize even the postwar border changes with Poland and Czechoslovakia, let alone the legitimacy of the East German state. Adenauer's policy toward the East, like his policy toward the West, was strongly resisted from within the Federal Republic. Indeed, some of the Christian Democratic opposition to Adenauer's European federalism was inspired by fears that it would foreclose German reunification. But however keen their nationalist sentiments, the liberal capitalists around Erhard were constrained from advocating a more adventurous reunification policy, both by their devotion to the American connection and by their antipathy toward communism. These self-defeating inhibitions were to become obvious in the CDU's *Ostpolitik* after Adenauer's departure. However, the Socialists, led initially by Kurt Schumacher, had opposed Adenauer's Eastern policy from the very beginning.

Schumacher was the third major figure of the recovery years. If Erhard represented the Atlantic option and Adenauer the European, Schumacher was the most obvious nationalist. His socialist convictions in no way led him to sympathize with the East German regime, let alone with its Russian patrons. Instead, he wanted a unified, social democratic Germany, disengaged from both superpowers and cultivating its own bloc of similar states in Central Europe. If Adenauer leaned toward a French-oriented continental policy, Schumacher favored a socialist, eastern-oriented version of *Mitteleuropa*. Because Schumacher's goal was unacceptable to Americans, Russians, other Europeans, and probably the majority of Germans, Adenauer's uncompromising Eastern policy prevailed easily throughout the Cold War period. But as the superpowers turned to detente, Adenauer's "hard line" seemed increasingly anachronistic to his American and European allies. Both the United States and the Soviet Union, fearful of nuclear confrontation, wanted to stabilize their respective European spheres through a mutual recognition of legitimacy. Divided Germany was the principal obstacle. Thus, each superpower had to persuade its Germany to recognize the other and, in effect, abjure reunification. For West Germany, with its large population of refugees, accommodation to detente was painful.

Germany's adjustment was pressed not only by the Americans, but also by the other Western Europeans, in particular the French. De Gaulle had his own ideas about detente. The Cold War should end, he argued, not with the stabilization of the superpower blocs in Europe, but with their disintegration. In the Gaullist prescription, Americans and Russians should cease confronting each other across the middle of Germany and start withdrawing to the periphery from whence they had come. A European system would then arise with its own center of gravity. Such a change would be a long process, de Gaulle admitted, moving through the stages of "detente, entente, and cooperation." In the long run, he mused, Russia itself might again be integrated into a European system, as its domestic and Asian problems hobbled its power in the West. In any event, de Gaulle believed European states should use detente to gain their freedom rather than consolidate their dependence. Detente "management" should therefore not be left a monopoly of the superpowers. European states should forge their own links with the Russians and with the other Eastern European countries. Only thus would the West Europeans have the possibility of freeing themselves from alien hegemonies and reestablishing their influence in the East.

French diplomacy pressed these ideas upon the Germans. German reunification could only take place, de Gaulle argued, within the autonomous Europe he envisioned. As long as Europe lay divided between two superpower systems, German reunification was impossible. In effect, de Gaulle's vision offered the Federal Republic national reunification within a Gallic version of the historic continental option. But Germany would have to attenuate its ties with the American world system. Two circles were enough.

Whatever the attractions for Adenauer of this Gallo-German Pan-Europa, he was not to remain in power long enough to pursue it. Instead, Erhard's foreign minister, Gerhard Schroeder – pro-American and anti-French – initiated his own Eastern policy, aimed apparently at undermining Russian influence by direct relations with other Eastern European countries. The same approach characterized the more active *Ostpolitik* of the Great Coalition that succeeded Erhard. Indeed, the Germans seemed to have taken up some of the Gaullist notions in a selective fashion that soon alarmed even the French. De Gaulle had seen a collective European policy, with France the interlocutor between Germany and the East. Not surprisingly, the Germans after Adenauer rejected French tutelage and seized the initiative for themselves. To the suspicious, the West Germans were hoping to use their economic power not only to ease the Russians out of Eastern Europe but to keep out the other Western Europeans as well. Whatever the validity of such apprehensions, Russia's invasion of Czechoslovakia in 1968, for which the French seemed to hold the Germans responsible, doubtless dampened whatever premature expectations the Germans may have been nourishing. But despite Czechoslovakia, the German diplomatic offensive soon revived. With the Social Democrats finally in power under Brandt's chancellorship, the federal Republic formally came to terms with the postwar European order.

Brandt was, if anything, more genuinely concerned with reunification than his predecessors. In some respects, he was the heir of Schumacher's early policy. But Brandt's nationalism was more tempered and realistic. Reunifying East and West Germany within a single nation-state was, he decided, impossible for the foreseeable future. After enjoying a disastrous interlude of unity under Hitler, the German nation was constrained to limit its union to the pre-Bismarckian formulas of Westphalia. But even so limited a form of reunification, Brandt believed, would be a great improvement over a Germany partitioned between two mutually antagonistic and alien-dominated blocs. Prolonging this status quo, particularly after the Berlin Wall was built, risked the loss of German national consciousness altogether.

Brandt's strategy assumed that to change the status quo Germany had first to recognize it. So the Federal Republic would have to accept formally the postwar changes, including a separate East German regime. But like de Gaulle, Brandt had a larger and dynamic vision of Europe's future.

Detente between the superpowers might, he argued, be manipulated into a "European Peace Order" – a looser Pan-European construction to replace the rigid postwar partition into blocs. The new order would have to be built in stages. Detente would first have to be consolidated into a European security system – a regulated coexistence (*geregeltes Nebeneinander*) organized around treaties renouncing force and limiting armaments in Central Europe. Both the United States and Russia would have to be engaged in this new structure, Brandt believed; hence, his Peace Order, unlike de Gaulle's, envisioned a continuing form of military hegemony for the superpowers. The military blocs would continue, but their relations would be stabilized and relaxed by a security system that was to engage them both. This new military stability, Brandt hoped, would permit a Pan-European organization for cooperation (*Organisierung des Miteinanders*). Economic, technological, and cultural collaboration among the European states would rebuild a Pan-European infrastructure and gradually constitute a "European Peace Order" or "European Peace Union." Peoples would move more freely; borders would become less significant; and some form of confederal, Pan-German construction would ultimately become feasible.

With Brandt in charge, the Federal Republic intensified its diplomatic offensive to the East. By 1972, treaties recognizing the postwar borders and promising nonaggression and cooperation had been signed and ratified with the Soviet Union, Czechoslovakia, Poland, and East Germany itself. Bonn recognized the postwar borders, while guarding the right to promote "peaceful change" and, in effect, recognized the German Democratic Republic as an independent state within a single German nation. Prompted by Bonn, the Four Powers signed a new agreement to settle the status of West Berlin and regulate the perennially vexing questions of access. With the German issues thus presumably settled, the way seemed open for talks on mutual and balanced force reductions" (MBFR), which in fact began in Vienna in 1972.

The way also lay open for Russia's cherished goal of a European Security Conference. Hence, in 1975, Europe gathered at Helsinki for a grand conference to mark the end of the Second World War. The consequent treaty had something for everyone. The superpowers celebrated their accommodation. The Gaullist view of detente, as well as Brandt's European Peace Order, found expression in various reaffirmations of national sovereignty as well as various Pan-European provisions to foster human rights, freedom of information, travel, and emigration.

Helsinki was followed by a period of disillusionment. Some expectations were obviously foolish. Each superpower seems to have expected a European detente to consolidate its own bloc and unravel its rival's. But detente could not resolve the internal problems of each sphere, most of which had little to do with outside subversion. Poland's economic problems were not creations of the CIA, any more than the economic, social, or political difficulties of Portugal, Spain, Italy, or Britain were caused by Moscow. As for Brandt's grand strategy, by 1978 neither side had yet seriously negotiated troop reductions – an unlikely and probably unwelcome prospect in any event. Instead, after Helsinki nearly all parties actually increased their conventional arms; even the strategic detente between the superpowers has remained uncertain.

And despite the hopes and promises of Helsinki, and the subsequent preoccupation of American policy with "human rights," the Eastern countries were scarcely thrown open to the free movement of peoples and ideas. At best, Eastern regimes evolved slowly toward a more liberal political climate, with the constant danger that instability would lead to major reversals. Economic ties did not continue their early rapid proliferation. As the foreign-exchange earnings of the communist states failed to keep peace with their appetites for imports, the glitter of Eastern trade grew dimmer. In the inner-German sphere, the old problems, if ameliorated, still continued. East Germany remained too unstable either to open its borders to the West or to relax significantly its repression at home. Maintaining ideological hostility remained a critical prop for the Eastern regime's legitimacy and, indeed, appeared more significant to the West German regime as well. In short, the GDR, allied with Russia, remained too strong for collapse, too protected for conquest, and still too weak for cooperation. West Germany's great diplomatic offensive seemed to have exhausted its possibilities.

With the stagnation of *Ostpolitik* after the mid-seventies, West Germany had explored its possibilities within the postwar order. The boundaries of the three circles had been measured thoroughly. The Federal Republic remained integrated within Atlantic and European systems and everything feasible had probably been done to foster ties with the East. Each sphere had been developed as far as possible without foreclosing the others. Further evolution of Germany's situation awaited further development within the postwar order generally. The Federal Republic had all along carefully avoided disturbing the essentials of that order. West Germany had merely sought to make the best of its position, short of challenging either superpower or abandoning the European coalition. And whatever its diplomatic disappointments, the Federal Republic had continued to prosper. Hence, the external constraints against a more adventurous or decisive German policy were reinforced by a strong disinclination to disturb arrangements that had proved so comfortable.

Whether the general trend of international events would continue to permit so comfortable and poised an indecision was becoming, by the late 1970s, the major question in Germany's future.

8

Germany in a More Plural World

The Erosion of the Postwar System

The Federal Republic's foreign policy has based itself upon three given factors: first, Russian hegemony over the east of Europe, including East Germany; second, the American "world" system, encompassing Western Europe, Japan, and most of the old colonial spheres; and finally, a Western European bloc within the American system. In each case, the Germans have always accommodated, often contributed, but never challenged. And, as an apparent compensation, they have prospered as never before in their history. What are the chances for changes in these given factors? What would be the likely consequences for Germany?

More than any other major nation, today's Germany reflects the international order of the postwar period. A divided Germany in a divided Europe is the direct creation of a bipolar world. Developments that lead away from that bipolarity could, of course, change significantly the possibilities open to German policy. But although experts have been predicting the end of bipolarity for a long time, it still persists in many essentials. In several respects, detente has actually stabilized bipolarity. In effect, the superpowers have made common cause in preserving the outlines of the postwar status quo, in Europe particularly. But the collapse of detente would most likely reinforce bipolarity even further. Although a renewed Cold War could conceivably allow one superpower to drive the other out of Europe, more probably, in a nuclear world, a new global confrontation would merely reinforce the superpowers in their respective European spheres, and most especially in their respective Germanies. Hence, the bipolar system is unlikely to end as a result of one superpower's victory over the other. The impulse away from bipolarity comes from changes within each sphere rather than from developments between them.

Such changes are more significant in the West than in the East. Russia's political, economic, and military power dwarfs the other states in its sphere and its domestic political culture poses few obstacles to heavy-handed military interventions in other countries. Hence, barring some cataclysmic domestic upheaval, Russian determination and strength seem more than adequate to hold the Soviet bloc together, despite its obvious stresses.

America's Western sphere, by contrast, is far more balanced. Western Europe's states, if not superpowers, nevertheless are populous, with highly developed economies, enormous wealth, worldwide connections, and considerable military prowess. Britain and France have elaborate nuclear forces of their own. Several other Western European states could easily have them as well. In one sense, the "West" constitutes a much stronger system, held together less by power than by myriad natural ties of interdependence. But, by the same token, no overwhelming force can be counted on to keep the Western or "Pan-Atlantic" system together, should its members grow seriously disenchanted. Nor is it certain that the United States itself is indefinitely committed to its own hegemonic role.

The American postwar system represents an extraordinary historical achievement. Thanks to it, the Western capitalist states have known three decades of unprecedented security, the foundation for one of the longest economic booms in modern history. But this Pax Americana was initially based on two rather unusual political conditions. The rest of the world was exceptionally weak and the United States was exceptionally assertive.

The war left most of Europe demoralized, disgraced, and in ruins. Europe's collapse, moreover, fatally weakened the old colonial order. Thus, outside the Soviet sphere, the United States was free to pursue its grand ambitions. Europe's autarchic nationalism and colonialism having been cleared away, Pax Americana was to modernize and restore the liberal dream of the last century. An Atlantic, and then "Pan-Atlantic" or "Trilateral"· community was to integrate the advanced capitalist nations into harmonious interdependence· Meanwhile, the "Third World" was to be "developed" to take its place within a liberal world system.

For the United States, these grand ambitions constituted an unusually assertive mood. Whereas the unbalanced economies of Britain and Germany had impelled them toward an imperial role, the United States remained a vast, secure, and autarchic continental power. The United States' enthusiasm for a world role flowed more from luxuriant ambition than intrinsic need.

Those two special postwar conditions, European weakness and American ambition, were historically unusual and not necessarily permanent. American opinion might have been expected to grow weary of imperial pretensions and burdens and a reviving Europe or "developing" Third World to grow restive at continuing American tutelage. Such developments could be expected to provoke and reinforce each other,· particularly in some period of general economic crisis.

All modern imperial systems may, in any event, have an

inherent tendency toward self-destruction, primarily because maintaining them may ultimately exhaust the hegemonic power. Britain's experience suggests a link between imperial burdens and domestic decay. Heavy arms expenditures and continual preoccupation with external problems may gradually erode the domestic base of the imperial power and, as one consequence, arouse antiimperialist forces at home. Should other powers challenge or start to pull away from the imperial orbit, the cost of maintaining the system grows. A heavier imperial burden calls for a heavier imperial tax for the services provided. Taxes may take various forms – direct military contributions from allies or economic concessions like artificial exchange rates, trade preferences, or increased military purchases. These demands may arouse further resistance from the allies, resistance that may, in turn, increase the leader's cost and strengthen its temptation to withdraw from the hegemonic role. Withdrawing from hegemony does not necessarily mean "isolationism" – a diminishing interest in the outside world. More likely, the hegemonic power begins to act more and more like a nation looking after its own particular national interests and less and less like the trustee for international order.

These abstract considerations have an obvious relevance to events in the past decade. Signs of a weakening imperial will in the United States have been visible since the 1960s when Vietnam made vivid the moral, military, and economic costs of the Pax Americana. Today, swelling domestic demands, both for public services and private investment, press upon the still-huge portion of America's national income channeled into an imperial military establishment. American economic policy seems increasingly oriented toward domestic priorities. Business and labor analysts worry about the high proportion of American capital directed abroad, the persistently low rate of capital investment in the United States relative to Europe and

Japan, and the long-range effects of technological transfer. Public opinion in general appears more skeptical of the advantages and propriety of foreign investment by America's multinational corporations. Domestic economic interests grow more assertive in demanding protection against foreign competition. These domestic concerns and forces have, in turn, powerfully influenced the United States' international monetary behavior. Since 1971, American governments have given up trying to constrain the domestic economy in the interests of a stable international monetary order. The learned apologetics of American economists not withstanding, Europeans, for the reasons discussed below, see the post-1971 monetary system as a particularly exploitative form of imperial taxation, an aggrandizement of American national interest at the expense of the international system as a whole.

As the cost of American protection has seemed to rise, its efficacy has declined. Soviet–American strategic parity makes the American military protectorate seem less reliable. Detente, Vietnam, and the Arab–Israeli conflict have all opened up contentious differences between the United States and its various allies. And since the oil embargo, Europe can no longer take for granted easy access to cheap supplies and developing markets. A more demanding and independent Third World squeezes Western prosperity and heightens competition among manufacturing nations. In an imperial system, when security grows more expensive and less certain, stronger nations begin to take their distance and look to their own needs. The international order again grows more Darwinian. Not surprisingly, political friction has grown steadily between the United States, Western Europe, and Japan.

If numerous signs point to an unraveling of the postwar American system, no one should be caught unawares. Transatlantic relations since the 1960s have been one long struggle to find a new relationship between Europe and the

THE GERMAN PROBLEM RECONSIDERED

United States. Normal recovery from the war was bound to increase Western Europe's political and economic weight in the transatlantic balance; its major states could be expected to grow restive at American hegemonic arrangements once accepted easily. Antihegemonic ideologies are always at hand to mobilize resistance. And although an integrated Western liberal order could, in theory, be continued without so overwhelming an American hegemony, the modalities have not been found. Conflict and disenchantment have grown rather than diminished. Thus, the adhesion of Europe and the United States has become more conditional and selective. Many believe, or hope, that the Pan-Atlantic system will adapt well enough to survive its present time of troubles. And so it may, because nearly everyone would prefer it. Still, mutual antagonism continues to grow, especially over economic problems, and nothing in the immediate future promises much relief.

The forms of European estrangement vary. Direct diplomatic conflicts flare up from time to time. More significant perhaps are domestic political changes closely tied to Europe's economic dissatisfaction. If leaders and parties who try to reconcile Atlanticist capitalism with the national welfare state go on failing to sustain growth and employment, or to control inflation, more radical governments will come forward. This trend should not be seen as some autonomous popular drift to radicalism, but as the consequence of a general undermining of Western economic and social stability by the years of "stagflation." Western governments find themselves less and less able to shape their national economic environments to counteract inflation and unemployment.

Throughout modern history, of course, most states have been powerless to rectify economic dislocations. But in the postwar era, the enlightened public has harbored the assumption that governments armed with Keynesian economics could influence national economic environments

well enough to avoid recurring crises. Recent years, however, have witnessed throughout the West a persistent and
increasingly destructive inflation, accompanied in the past
few years by tenacious unemployment. Fashionable analysis blames inflation on domestic or international expectations that outstrip productivity – irresponsible wage
demands, self-indulgent consumerism, or the vaulting
ambition of oil producers. The roots of the current monetary malaise, however, go back well beyond both the oil
crisis and the European wage explosions of the late sixties.
As early as 1965, for example, the French government
launched a major attack on American international monetary deficits as "inflationary." The French analysis of the
inflationary mechanism has grown difficult to dispute. The
gold-exchange standard, with its inadequate sanctions
against American deficits, has certainly proved inherently
unstable and inflationary. But a more comprehensive view
must also note how American exchange deficits were natural by-products of the overall political-economic system.
Any practical analysis of American deficits throughout
the fifties to the mid-sixties cannot ignore how much they
stemmed from the exchange costs of America's foreign aid,
military commitments, or corporate investment. This outflow, it may easily be argued, was essential for maintaining
the existing international political-economic system. The
deficits arose because, even after Europe had recovered,
the United States was not being adequately compensated
for its imperial services. In short, the international monetary disequilibrium, which, as the French observed, could
hardly help but fuel inflation, did not originate merely
from accumulating domestic excesses, but also from a
more fundamental systemic disequilibrium – an imbalance
between the economic resources and political responsibilities of Europe and the United States.

Since 1971, calculations of international monetary balance have been sophisticated both by a floating dollar and

by the immense pool of accumulated American debts held abroad. This latter has been organized into the Eurodollar market, a great volatile mass of liquid capital that now finances, in its turn, the mounting debts of several other countries. In one fundamental respect, the new floating monetary system is the same as the old: Nothing compels adjustment. No sanctions, economic or political, are sufficient to induce major countries, deficit or surplus, to adopt policies leading to equilibrium. In particular, Americans still run whatever deficits they please. For so long as the dollar remains the world's only feasible reserve currency, the United States can expect others to finance much of its deficit by holding dollars in their reserves. And whenever they do balk and the dollar falls, the United States' huge and relatively autarchic economy gives it relative insulation from the inflationary consequences of the devaluing. With imports and exports so small in relation to our GNP, devaluation affects American domestic prices far less than in the average European country. Under the circumstances, "adjustment," insofar as it has really occurred, has been at the expense of European competitiveness. For as the dollar depreciates, American manufactures tend to grow relatively attractive. The effects have been remarkable. In 1971, 14.1 percent of all goods produced in the United States were exported. By 1974, the ratio was nearly 24 percent, and remained nearly as high through 1977.

This form of "adjustment" was hardly pleasing to the Europeans, particularly in a period of general economic stagnation. Nor was it easy to see any relief in the future. For despite the great increase in exports, the United States' trade deficit was greatly expanded in the 1970s by a growing thirst for imported oil. American oil imports increased from $1.5 billion in 1960, to $2.8 billion in 1970, to $34.2 billion in 1976, to around 40 billion in 1977. In European eyes, American profligacy, having first created

conditions in the oil market that made possible the quadru-
pling of prices, has condemned Europeans to a choice
between overvalued currencies or inflation. Because oil is
factored in dollars, and Saudi Arabia is an American military protectorate, nothing restrains the United States from
importing as much oil as it pleases. The resulting "petro-
dollars" either return to the United States, or make their
way to Europe, where they pose the old dilemma.

With trade and monetary flows increasingly unpredictable and politicized, nationalist pressures for outright protectionism mount everywhere, not least in the United States
itself. The new protectionism of the 1970s reflects a fundamental paradox of the postwar American system. As the
system has moved toward an ever closer interdependence, it
has become progressively more unstable. The liberalization
of trade and investment, enhanced and conditioned by the
growth of multinational enterprise, has gradually deprived
national governments of those Keynesian instruments that
were meant to control their economies. Hence the growing
fear that the bad old days of unmanageable capitalism have
returned. With both free trade in goods and massive and
rapid international movements of capital, national monetary and fiscal policies no longer work effectively. Hence
the almost universal nationalist impulse to withdraw into
protectionism. If depressed and uncertain conditions continue, radical new forces, determined to reassert national
control, will grow stronger. Existing governments and parties, to survive, will be constrained to move with the nationalist forces. No one, of course, should assume that the new
nationalism will necessarily spring only from the Left.
Whatever its political base, it will be sustained and driven
by the need to regain control of domestic economic environments that have become intolerable to the average citi-
zen. National systems will increasingly tend to dissociate
from a world economy that continually threatens domestic
welfare and stability. Like Chamberlain and Roosevelt in

the 1930s, not to mention Hitler, political leaders will come to prefer greater autarchy to an unmanageable internationalism. Such an evolution points to a more protectionist European system, relatively dissociated from that version of liberal international capitalism characteristic of recent years. In short, if present trends continue, centrifugal nationalist forces will increasingly threaten the postwar American system, even within its transatlantic core.

Germany in a Troubled World:
Economic Consequences

How does this direction of world forces affect West Germany? Because the postwar world order has been particularly good to the Federal Republic, and especially to its economy, Bonn has, in many respects, become the principal ally of the United States in sustaining that order. And so far the general economic malaise has probably touched West Germany less than any other major European economy. Nevertheless, the Germans are deeply troubled and political friction between German and American governments has mounted steadily throughout the later seventies. The Germans have not forgotten their essential vulnerability. And despite the long duration of their postwar prosperity, they increasingly fear its loss.

To begin with, Germany's postwar economic development has not been as untroubled as is sometimes imagined. Although American security and the long postwar boom provided exceptionally favorable circumstances, success was not automatic for Europe's economies, as can be inferred from the fate of Britain, Germany's historic archrival. The West German economy passed from its desolation at the war's end, through a painful reconstruction, to its "miracle" of the fifties. For the reasons discussed above, the Federal Republic was exceptionally well-suited to profit from the boom induced by Europe's recovery in general and the Korean War in particular.

German economic progress first began to slacken by the mid-sixties. A downturn in the international economy showed many German firms to have grown rather careless. Moreover, since the Berlin Wall had ended mass immigration from the East in 1961, labor was growing short and the era of the less assimilable *Gastarbeiter* beginning. Nevertheless, by the late sixties, Germany's recession was mostly over. Labor unions had cooperated to keep wages down, companies had returned to higher profit margins and more competitive world prices. Strict government policies had helped to keep German inflation well below that of other major exporters. The German mark once more became an undervalued currency. Tight money and labor discipline had again given Germany a substantial advantage in world markets.

The beginning of the seventies, however, brought renewed difficulties. The elections of 1969 and 1972 produced Willy Brandt's Social Democratic–Free Democratic coalition, a government committed to more generous social and labor policies. With business profits rebounding, unions demanded major wage increases, including compensation for their restraint in the recession years. Thus, in 1970, average monthly wage rates rose by more than 15 percent – the highest rate of increase since the Korean War. In many industries, shorter work hours and higher benefits raised the labor bill over 20 percent.

At the same time as higher wages threatened to undermine competitiveness, strong international pressure was forcing the German mark to appreciate. Formal revaluations against the dollar and other major European currencies occurred in 1969, 1971, and 1973. Germany's trade surplus with the European Community of DM1,823 million in 1970 had become a deficit of DM3,169 million by 1972.

The year 1973 brought the energy crisis, which disrupted the world economy and many of Germany's export markets. Paradoxically, however, West Germany was injured less than most other European countries. With still huge coal reserves, the Federal Republic depended relatively less upon oil. Moreover, with several newly rich oil states – like Iran – using their augmented revenues to build industry and infrastructure, Germany's export-oriented capital-goods industry was a prime beneficiary. Nevertheless, with the Common Market countries absorbing over half the Federal Republic's exports, Germany's prosperity was unlikely to survive prolonged economic and political malaise among its neighbors. And, insofar as the oil crisis pointed to the gradual disintegration of the American world system, it reminded the Germans of their own dependence and vulnerability.

Hence, as the seventies have progressed, a sort of low-grade crisis of confidence has afflicted the German economy. But with the Federal Republic's huge monetary reserves, formidable trade surplus, low inflation rate, and impressive national statistics in general, foreigners tend to find German fears extravagant. Many foreign experts, in the United States particularly, accuse the Germans of beggaring their neighbors. The huge trade surplus seems an affront to Germany's partners. West Germany, it is said, should stimulate its domestic economy to increase its imports and thus aid recovery throughout the rest of the system.

Whatever the correctness of Germany's short-term policies, the fears for the future are not without foundation. Although relative "productivity" is notoriously difficult to measure, Germany's does seem to be declining. Numerous discouraging factors are frequently cited. Germany's labor situation is less promising than heretofore. After the Berlin Wall shut off the flow of refugees, new labor came increasingly from non-German immigrants. By 1973, West Germany employed 2.6 million non-Germans, close to 10 percent of the labor force. By the mid-seventies, the social costs of this immigrant labor began to be reckoned a major burden on finances and civility. In a Social Democratic welfare state, foreign workers could not be denied equal public benefits and educational advantages. But educational and housing facilities have become increasingly stretched. In the later seventies, heavy unemployment has strained the welfare system's finances.

A growing consensus has demanded a gradual reduction of foreign labor. Immigration has stopped and companies have used recessionary periods to buy out their foreign workers on a substantial scale. By the end of 1975, foreign labor had declined to 2.04 million – down 21 percent from its peak in 1973. Experts project a stabilized level of 1.6 million by 1980.

As an obvious consequence, labor can be expected to grow scarcer and the pressure on wages to increase. German wages, of course, are already very high. Indeed, since 1970, they have increased astronomically, particularly when comparative inflation rates and currency changes are taken into account. Whereas labor's demands once more grew relatively restrained with the recession in the mid-seventies, businessmen fear renewed militancy and, in any event, rates have already risen more substantially than among Germany's major competitors (see Table 3).

Unless higher wage costs can be passed on through higher prices, they obviously tend to squeeze company

Table 3. *Manufacturing Unit Labor Costs* (in U.S. dollars, 1967 = 100)

	Germany	U.S.A.	Japan	France	Italy	Neth.	U.K.
1960	78.1	97.7	82.7	81.7	76.5	65.4	85.7
1970	124.6	116.5	106.0	98.9	119.2	108.4	106.0
1976	249.3	156.9	180.7	188.5	213.2	N.A.	180.7

Source: U.S. Department of Commerce, *International Economic Indicators*, December 1977, p. 86.

profits. But German companies have been constrained from price increases by the antiinflationary bias of government policy, and, above all, by the dramatically appreciating German mark. From September 1969 to March 1978, the DM appreciated approximately 81 percent against the dollar, 25 percent against the yen, 63 percent against the French franc, 145 percent against the pound, and 164 percent against the lira. German exports clearly did not suffer correspondingly. Why not?

Conventional economic wisdom notes that Germany's relatively low inflation rate, which encourages currency appreciation, also helps keep export prices competitive. And products like capital goods are not so price-sensitive, it is said. Another explanation, however, is also common in German business circles. German exporters have traditionally emphasized volume – especially in heavy industry where volume is closely correlated with profit. With the currency appreciating, volume has been maintained by a declining markup. Hence, profit rates in many large German export-oriented firms have fallen precipitously since the sixties. Recovery since 1975 has still not brought overall industrial profit rates back to the growth level of the sixties. Moreover, because the steady rise in capital-goods prices in recent years means that conventional data understate replacement costs, the improvement in profit position is probably exaggerated.

Low profits and potential labor shortages naturally discourage domestic business investment, constrained anyway in a crowded country by a growing sensitivity to environmental costs. Discouraging domestic prospects, combined with an appreciating currency, favor investment abroad. Foreign investment may improve the profits of German firms, but low domestic investment only further erodes productivity. And as German costs rise, unless "high technology" replaces heavy industry, Germany's industrial base seems fated to decay. Hence, the frequently heard complaint among Germans that their economy has "matured" and is starting on Britain's path to decline.

This discouraging "maturation" has taken place against a backdrop of world recession, and a corresponding slowing of international trade. With traditional markets in Western Europe particularly hard-hit, and with all the problems of their appreciating currency, the Germans have had to scramble for new markets. Their success has been impressive first with the Soviet bloc and then with the oil-producing or other industrializing countries of the Third World. But much of this success is qualified by its increasingly precarious financial base. German export terms, as in Clapham's day, continue to astonish the world. But as a result, they now hold an uncomfortably large debt from many of their new customers. In effect, West Germany has been using its accumulated monetary surplus to finance employment in its export industries. As the debt of several major customers reaches the outer limits of prudence, the impressive balancing act of recent years may come to a close.

Finally, although the German balance of payments seems almost the strongest in the world, a closer look reveals some long-range perils. For the economy and society are now structured to a large foreign outflow for services, transfers to families of immigrant workers, capital investment, and tourism. Should the compensating trade surplus begin to falter, the overall payments could turn strikingly negative. It may be more difficult to "fine tune" Germany's balance of payments than fashionable critics of German policy apparently believe. In any event, we may soon see. The German government, prodded by the United States, has gradually abandoned those frugal habits upon which its low inflation has been based. From 1970 to 1977, the annual deficit of the West German federal government grew from DM1,400 million to DM21,000 million. For 1978, the predicted deficit was

DM28,000 million, a figure equal to 3 percent of the GNP. When other public-sector deficits are added in, the projected deficit grows to DM52,000 million, 4 percent of the expected GNP. The comparable ratio for the U.S. public-sector deficit is expected to be a little over 1 percent.

In summary, with all the uncertainties of their domestic and international environment, the prosperous Germans grow increasingly troubled. Inevitably, any analysis of their economic future is conjectural. Nevertheless, the general malaise of the Western system has affected the Germans more than it might seen. A long period of economic stagnation in a fragmenting world political-economic system would find them dangerously exposed. The Germany that never gained an empire may lose its comfortable postwar role. Small wonder if Germans with long memories grow nervous.

Germany's Choices for the Future

If the postwar system continues to disintegrate, what is Germany's future? So prosperous and vulnerable a country has an understandable impulse to help shore up the system. Fashionable transatlantic opinion calls for an even closer partnership with the United States – a "bigemony" – or a "trilateral" directorate with the United States and Japan. It is understandable why the United States might be interested in promoting such an arrangement – the newest version of the multilateral hocus-pocus by which we have governed the postwar world. But Germany's economic interest is less clear. The general European–American trade competition has already been discussed. The German mark and Japanese yen are the principal victims of America's exchange policies. Moreover, as the German economy becomes more "mature," German trade will presumably find its future in high technology. There the Americans are still preeminent and, as the various continuing quarrels over nuclear reactor sales suggest, mutual accommodation may be difficult. In short, increasingly sharp economic competition bodes ill for a special German–American partnership. More likely, bigemony will at best serve to divert the Germans from a forthright European policy.

The European option, like the Atlantic, also poses great difficulties for the West Germans. However diverting their transatlantic ties, Germans cannot easily ignore the close link between their prosperity and the European market. The Federal Republic cannot easily flourish in a prolonged European depression. Nor can the Federal Republic easily isolate itself from the political trends of its neighbors. With tension growing between the United States and the rest of Europe, what is happening to the postwar continental option?

In theory, a Western Europe relatively dissociated from the United States would have even more reason to cling together. A collective European system, extended to the south, might prove a tolerable substitute for the postwar transatlantic system. But could a confederal European coalition stand the strain – both of transition to more nationalist governments, perhaps of diverse ideological foundations, and of estrangement from the United States? No one can speak with great assurances about questions based on so many hypothetical assumptions. However, certain general observations about European solidarity seem appropriate to consider.

If a number of radical governments came to power, ideological diversity could easily threaten Europe's cohesion. The European coalition built around the Common Market would have trouble accommodating marked deviations from liberal economic practices. A Leftist or Neo-Gaullist regime in France, for example, might find itself unable to control multinationals while remaining within the European Community. The temptation to unilateral action and autarchic controls would be strong, especially for a new government with radical pretensions. Problems of mutual accommodation would severely tax the skills of European diplomacy.

Europeans have also always been divided by their differing perceptions of dependence upon the United States. Among the European states, West Germany is not only the most economically successful within the postwar system, but also perhaps the most vulnerable to disruption. Moreover, West Germany senses itself the most dependent upon American military protection. Hence the West Germans have been far less willing to challenge American hegemony in various spheres than the French. But the Germans have seldom been alone in their steadfast Atlantic loyalty. Thus, even if most European states inclined toward a more independent European system, European unity might well still fragment over a hard policy toward the United States.

With so many cleavages of particular national interests and conditions, plus all the complications of different directions and rates of change in the various states, Europe's coalition would be difficult to sustain in seriously troubled times. In such circumstances, Europe would perhaps hold together only if one power were able to predominate. Might the Federal Republic, to save its continental option, be forced to bid for active hegemony within the European Community? If so, Germany's prospects would be problematical. The ability to impose its will on Europe is strictly limited. The Federal Republic has the largest population, economy, and trade. But France and even Britain are not so much smaller and have diplomatic and military assets denied the Germans. Moreover, Germany's will to pay the price for leadership also seems rather limited. Indeed, from a certain current German view, the Federal Republic, despite the manifest benefits it derives from the European Community, is already Europe's "milk cow," the subsidizer of everyone else's financial excesses and social weaknesses.

Of course, success at hegemony cannot be reckoned apart from the policies advocated, nor from the general framework within which leadership is meant to be exercised. A Germany that was an exponent of "European" as opposed to "Atlantic" interests might be more acceptable a leader than a Germany, bemused by "bigemony" which sought to be the European spokesman for American interests. Europe's coalition, of course, has always rested upon a Franco-German entente. Neither could "lead" without the acquiescence of the other. But in a major crisis with the United States, even the two principal states together could not necessarily make their joint will prevail. In any event, French and German interests do not appear to be growing more harmonious. France, for example, has proved neither willing nor able to sustain fixed exchange rates with Germany's appreciating mark. Behind this particular failure in partnership lie not only differing national economic interests and capabilities, but opposing conceptions of international monetary order and, ultimately, of Europe's proper relationship to the United States. To lead a Europe that includes France, Germany would presumably have to become more "European" or France more "Atlantic." But in the face of a strong German drive for European hegemony, how anti-American would France, Britain, or the lesser powers remain? Much, of course, would depend on the quality of German leadership. Neither the remote nor recent past gives cause for easy optimism.

If Germany cannot lead Europe, it must inevitably be tempted to play a national rather than European game. With its industry heavily oriented toward exports of capital goods, the Federal Republic has had impressive success in the developing economies of Eastern Europe and the Third World. By diversifying in these directions, Germany could hope for a way to sustain its prosperity in relative independence from a troubled European or Atlantic system. But, as noted above, these prospects, if important, are also limited. The developing Third World needs capital machinery but many of its countries lack the financial means to pay for it. And once the machinery is installed and functioning, there will be the question of reciprocity in German markets. Germany may, of course, become a *rentier* society, living off foreign income generated by manufacturing investments in other countries. But many things will have to change in Germany before such an evolution becomes manageable. Moreover, *rentier* empires are for the strong and Germans lack the military power to sustain an imperial role. And it seems less probable that Germans can count indefinitely upon a benevolent American imperium. In short, although Germany will inevitably try to develop further an independent world economic position, it is unlikely to provide an economic alternative to Europe, or, for that matter, a political alternative to "Atlantica." Germany is too big to become either a Switzerland or a Sweden. Its costs are already too high to be a Japan. It remains too good at industry to become a Britain.

There remains the old dream of a partnership with Russia. But the military and political hazards of such a relationship are obvious. And it seems unlikely that the Russians would be content to become, once again, the hinterland for German industry. Clearly, both Germans and Russians are far from such a special relationship today. How might such a relationship evolve, and what would be its attractions for Germany?

The combination of supposed American weariness with imperial burdens and the rise of Leftist forces in several countries has inspired a fashionable gloom about Europe's future. According to this view, European societies are in the throes of a self-indulgent phase of social democracy. Leftist governments, with important or even dominant communist participation, will take power in France and in Italy, also perhaps in Spain and Portugal. The United States will grow increasingly alienated and withdrawn. Rus-

sian influence will grow. West Germany will find itself
increasingly isolated – abandoned by the Americans, surrounded by an uncongenial Western Europe, and menaced
by the Russians. In such circumstances, it is said, the Federal Republic, along with the rest of Western Europe, will
be "Finlandized," by which is meant that European states
will somehow accommodate themselves to Soviet military
hegemony and attach their economies to the Soviet system.

  Not everyone would look upon these prospects with total
dismay. For Germans with an adventurous turn of mind,
"Finlandization" might come to seem the best chance for
national reunification and revival – more promising, it
must seem, than hopes for a Russian collapse or for a gradual Eastern evolution to liberalism. With both Germanies
in a common system, division would lose its original rationale and be far more difficult to sustain. Russia's hegemonic
power might more easily be contained, even as it appeared
to triumph. A socialist Europe from the Atlantic to the
Urals would be much more balanced than the present
Soviet system. And if unified, Germany – under whatever
government – would soon exert enormous national weight,
even within a Soviet-led system. In short, the Federal
Republic, faced with the collapse of both its Atlantic and
European options, might find the way to reunification
through an apparent Soviet victory in Europe. With Germany united, it might be hoped, Western Europe and the
Soviet Union could then form a viable new system,
sufficiently balanced to prevent Soviet exploitation.

  The hope for such an evolution seems unrealistic for the
very reasons that might seem to make it attractive. Western
Europe, even if estranged from the United States, would
still be too large and powerful a group of states to be
absorbed easily into the Soviet system. How would it be
possible for the Soviets to enter into intimate economic
relations with the dynamic societies of Western Europe?
Perhaps another European war might reduce the Western

states to a sufficiently dismal dependence. But for the usual nuclear reasons, such a European war seems highly improbable. And if it comes, the Russians themselves are not likely to be spared while Europe is ruined. In any event, a Russian system would not only have great trouble incorporating Western Europe in general, but particularly serious difficulty in accommodating a united Germany. Indeed, few developments would probably be less welcome to the Kremlin than a friendly communist government in Bonn.

To bring these speculations to a close: In a disintegrating postwar system no obvious course imposes itself upon Germany. The old European option, although perhaps the most promising, bristles with difficulties. The prospects for an independent Germany seem strictly limited. And special relations with either superpower are likely to founder on the economic and political realities of Germany's place in the world.

Conclusions: Germany in a Disintegrating World Order

Germany in the postwar era has not lost its traditional concerns – even if they have now taken new forms. Both postwar German states approximate the world or "Little German" models. Both have escaped from the traditional problems of that option by participating within a large-scale, political-economic system maintained by a superpower. Both have done well within the limitations imposed by those systems. The principal cost has been their division.

West Germany has been able to maneuver within the Atlantic system far more freely than East Germany within the Soviet. Inside the American-sponsored order, a European economic bloc has grown up that gives the Federal Republic the possibility of reviving, in partnership with its neighbors, a Pan-European version of the old continental model. Tensions between this European bloc and America's hegemonic order were inherent at the start and have grown more conscious and severe in recent years. So far, Germany has successfully resisted being forced to choose between these two Western systems – a choice not merely between the United States and France, or the United States and Europe, but also between the traditional world and continental models for Germany's future. Instead of choosing, West Germany has enjoyed the best of both. In effect, Germany has played an important balancing role. Were it not for the reunification issue, West Germany would have little reason to fault the postwar order. As it is, German efforts to develop the possibilities for reunification have remained carefully compatible with world and continental opinions. The Federal Republic has never challenged the postwar system in any of these spheres. Instead, Germany has carefully balanced Atlantic, European, and independent national policies. Although priority has shifted, Germany has drawn back whenever one policy has threatened the others. It is difficult, then, to count West Germany as a revisionist power toward the postwar system.

Recent years, however, have put increasing strain on that postwar order, particularly in the West. An expected restiveness of a reviving Europe under American tutelage has been reinforced by several other trends. A serious faltering in the long postwar boom has led to a new climate of heightened competition among the Western capitalist states. Increasing demands from the Third World have appeared to jeopardize Western economic security and prosperity. American will and capacity to continue guaranteeing and "managing" the system have seemed diminished, not only by external resistance but also by nationalist sentiments in the United States. All these conditions have tended to push European states into more active and independent policies. A certain revival of the old geopolitical arguments about competition between European states and the United States is to be expected. Along with this revival should logically come a strengthening of bonds among the European states, a certain disengagement of Europe and the United States, and a more plural world system generally.

That the European states could sustain their own cohesion through such an evolution is, however, far from certain. Among the European states, differing economic interests, ideological commitments, domestic political trends and styles, Atlantic loyalties, and military dependence all make a breakup of effective European cooperation quite imaginable, even if Europe's long-range common interest is widely perceived and admitted.

In summary, even if increasing tensions make preservation of the postwar status quo more and more difficult, West Germany has no clear alternative. Each of its Atlantic, European, or nationalist options has serious liabilities. The future, in short, is highly uncertain; the next thirty years are unlikely to be as tranquil as the last. Under increasing pressure, German politics may well grow more and more uneasy and strident.

In the postwar era, the Germans have had a sort of vacation from their traditional problems. Should that era end and old problems return, as seems not unlikely, West Germany can hardly escape a crucial role in the evolution of Atlantic and European systems. The Germans will once more actively shape their own destiny. Germans have not met such challenges with notable success in the past. This time, perhaps, the prospects are more promising.

A common European solution could, in theory, resolve the old economic dilemma without isolating Germany or pushing it into new and possibly disastrous adventures. But what future role Germany will play in building a European coalition is as unpredictable as it is important. Against Germany's obvious European interest is the discouraging weakness and division of its partners, the competing lures of its own national aggrandizement and reunification, as well perhaps as its traditional cultural inwardness, insecurity, and diplomatic ineptitude. Even its admirers must wonder if Germany is ready. If not, Germany may fail once again. And Europe, instead of a new world power, may become a graveyard for old states.

9

The German Problem and its Lessons

German intellectuals in the last century were infatuated with the classical world to the point where cultural historians can speak of a Greek "tyranny" over the German imagination. Germans were held in thrall not only by the measured beauty of Apollo but also by the mad energy of Dionysus. Indeed, it was the latter's wild, undisciplined force that was reborn in those rude Norse gods so popular with the German public. Consciously or unconsciously, the Germans almost seem to have made their history a modern Greek tragedy. The principal characters do seem cut to mythic dimensions. Bismarck was a haunted giant, hustled by fate, his indomitable will facing down the doom that he anticipated. Bethmann-Hollweg was the archetype of the modern bureaucratic politician — tirelessly patching, infinitely resourceful in avoiding the inevitable, quietly desperate, driven finally to a cosmic gamble. And Hitler, for all the pornography of Nazi politics, was possessed by a terrible elemental force that carried Germany to adventure and ruin awesome enough for any mythic tale.

If German history is a modern tragedy, what is its

lesson? Is there a fatal flaw that makes the ruin rational and thereby confirms the world's moral order? Does modern Germany illustrate, as de Gaulle said of Napoleon, the "tragic revenge of measure [and] just wrath of reason"?

Preceding chapters have examined many aspects of the German tragedy. Their broad conclusion seems clear. The German Problem does not somehow emanate from some special German "character." Imperial Germany was not uniquely aggressive, only uniquely inconvenient. Whatever faults and ambitions the Germans had were amply shared by the other major nations of the modern era. But unlike Britain, Russia, or the United States, the Germans lacked the space to work out their abundant vitality. Moreover, because of geography, Germany's vitality was an immediate threat to the rest of Europe. Modern Germany was born encircled. Under the circumstances, whatever the lesson of the wars between Germany and its neighbors, it cannot be found merely by analyzing the faults of the Germans.

The Germans, in fact, were not so different from their British, French, and Russian neighbors. All four, as they have become modern nation-states, have shown an astonishing, "aggressive" vitality, which has carried their national power far beyond the limited confines of their homelands. The Germans, moreover, share many traits with the Americans, perhaps because so many Americans have German ancestors. Like the United States, Germany underwent a late and very rapid growth, characterized above all by an extraordinary talent for large-scale organization. Like the Americans, the Germans were latecomers to world politics, often arrogant in their new power, insular and unmeasured in their ambitions. Unlike the Americans, however, the Germans lacked a continental backyard. They also lacked the Anglo-Saxon talent for cant, which, no doubt, explains their relative lack of success at propaganda, not least among historians. More fatally, the Germans have lacked the American talent for hegemony. Perhaps the American domestic experience has been better training for imperial power. Long before the polyglot United States grew to world power, its elites had had to learn at home how to accommodate subordinate but proud peoples. Anyone who can govern the United States can probably govern the world. By contrast, German domestic society was more efficient and less exasperating, hence poor training for world management.

In any event, whatever its similarities with the other great powers, Germany has found nearly all of them ranged against it in the two decisive battles of the century. Not surprisingly, the Germans have lost their battles. In the end, the real victors have been the United States and Russia. The European Great Powers, Britain, France, and Germany, now share a common demotion. Like the French, the Germans have lost their bid for continental hegemony, and like the British, they have lost their hope for world power. In today's world of the superpowers, all three have become secondary powers, rich and vulnerable. Nevertheless, reports of the imminent death of Europe's nation-states have proved premature. Like aging sopranos, they refuse to retire. Their technique remains impressive even if their voices grow feebler and their repertory more restricted. Moreover, as the world grows more plural, traditional nation-states may enjoy a certain revival. Technique and agility may count for more and size for less. In any event, Pan-Europa is still very much alive – its survival in adversity in some respects as impressive as its achievements in prosperity. In short, the German tale may not yet be told.

Before speculating about the future, what remains to be said of the past? If Germany was not so different from the others, what then is the lesson of the great wars of this century? The answer, in my view, is not very startling for students of human nature and history: Accelerating national ambitions, fed by the vaulting expectations of rapidly growing but unstable societies, make international conflict nearly inevitable.

All modern societies have been touched by the Faustian dream of an infinite power over nature. Modern man is no longer resigned to his limitations. Great as the achievements are, the ambitions grow faster. And the ambitions are transferred, moreover, from one society to the next. In those periods when technology and general circumstances permit rapid growth, an international system can accommodate these universally rising expectations. When that growth is seen to falter, the international climate grows Darwinian. Thwarted domestic expectations seek refuge in power and conflicts grow increasingly unmanageable. In these circumstances, democracy proves to be not a cure but an aggravation. No despot is more demanding than a powerful people deprived of its newly won prosperity.

Since the middle of the last century, the world has known three long cycles of headlong growth followed by prolonged periods of contraction and squeeze. Attempts to protect national economies in these oscillations have ultimately created problems too great for peaceful adjustment among states. Seen from this perspective, Germany's tragedy becomes the problem of modern society in general. Of all the great modern nations, Germany has been the most vulnerable. When the pressures on the system have been ready to explode, Germany has been the flashpoint.

Where then are we now? The similarities between our present predicament and this broad analysis of the past are all too obvious. The latest postwar era has been an unprecedented period of rapid real growth and an even more rapid growth of expectations. Unfulfillable ambition is no longer a Western luxury. New states revel in new growth and power, and dream those fatal dreams once limited to the West. The unmeasured ambition of the new states now competes with the inflated pretensions of the old. Unfortunately, as expectations have risen, growth has declined. The world economy has now entered what appears to be a prolonged period of relative restraint. Our present inflation reflects a transitional phase where unreconstructed expectations confront shrinking resources. It is inevitably a time for manipulators – clever fixers whose task is increasingly desperate. The temptation to grab resources at the expense of the international system as a whole becomes ever more compelling. Hence, as we have seen, the steady growth of an aggressive neomercantilism among all states – the United States not least – and a steady deterioration in the general climate of political and economic relations among states, notably among the United States, Europe, and Japan.

For the historic pessimist, the end of the story is not beyond prediction. Sooner or later, tension will explode into violence. Whether it takes the form of domestic revolution or old-fashioned war, whether it is between East and West, North and South, or, as before, West and West, will no doubt depend, as much as anything, upon the accidents and machinations of statecraft.

Is Germany still a major flashpoint? The Germans will likely do their best to avoid being, once more, the center of a general world catastrophe. But, divided as they are, and in the midst of a restive Europe, history may strike them yet again. No doubt, they should study their past to avoid, if they can, yet another repetition. But, as the preceding chapters may suggest, it is not only the Germans who should study the German Problem. For it is not to Germany that we would go today to find the most egregious examples of ambitions outrunning resources, nor it might be argued, is it the Germans whose arrogant failure to adjust to a new world strains the international system beyond endurance.

Bibliographical Essay

The bibliography that follows is in no sense a comprehensive survey of the vast body of scholarship that exists on the subjects of my various essays. Rather, it is an acknowledgment of the principal sources and analyses to which I feel most indebted. As I mention in Chapter 1, my essays break no new ground in primary-source materials dealing with modern German history; instead, they reexamine familiar events in new perspectives. To some extent, these perspectives arise from the waning of the intense anti-German emotions of the Second World War. More fundamentally, they spring from a search in prewar history for the likely consequences of an end to postwar duopoly. In a sense, this work responds to the call in Geoffrey Barraclough's *Introduction to Contemporary History* (New York: Basic Books, 1965) for a fresh look at the past in the light of the new world that has been emerging since 1945. To be sure, I lack Barraclough's grasp of German history and I am perhaps more inclined to see the continuities between the "modern" era before 1945 and the "contemporary" era that has been emerging since. As detente,

211

disaffection between Europe and the United States, and the rise of the Third World all ostensibly make the international system more "plural," the fundamental problems of the state system before the Second World War seem more rather than less relevant. This new climate may, moreover, give us new insights into those fundamental traditional problems.

I am generally indebted to Ludwig Dehio's *Germany and World Politics in the Twentieth Century* (New York: Knopf, 1959) and *The Precarious Balance: Four Centuries of the European Power Struggle* (New York: Knopf, 1962). No one shows better how the historical imagination can escape the distorting conventions of its immediate surroundings. Something of the same magisterial detachment can be found in Hajo Holborn's collection of essays, *Germany and Europe* (Garden City, N.Y.: Doubleday, 1970), which provides insight into an extraordinary range of topics. Another learned and stimulating attempt to look at German history in broader perspective can be found in Andreas Hillgruber's essay, *Kontinuität und Diskontinuität in der deutschen Aussenpolitik von Bismarck bis Hitler* (Düsseldorf: Droste, 1969). Finally, although I dispute various of his conclusions throughout this work, I should acknowledge my general debt to A. J. P. Taylor's remarkable writings on modern Germany, in particular his *Origins of the Second World War* (London: Hamilton, 1961), *The Course of German History* (London: Hamilton, 1945), and *Bismarck, the Man and the Statesman* (London: Hamilton, 1955). Taylor's frequent review articles are, in themselves, a continual source of fresh and penetrating analysis.

Imperial Germany: Politics and Diplomacy

For my essay on Bismarck, I have found particularly helpful the following: A. J. P. Taylor, *Bismarck, the Man and the Statesman* (London: Hamilton, 1955); Alan Palmer,

Bismarck (London: Weidenfeld and Nicolson, 1976)
Erich Eyck, *Bismarck and the German Empire* (3rd ed.;
London: Unwin University Books, 1968); Otto Pflanze,
Bismarck and the Development of Modern Germany
(Princeton, N.J.: Princeton University Press, 1963); W. N.
Medlicott, *Bismarck and Modern Germany* (London: English Universities Press, 1965); and W. M. Simon, *Germany in the Age of Bismarck* (London: Allen and Unwin, 1968).
Taylor particularly emphasizes the conservatism and
Prussian orientation of Bismarck's later foreign and
domestic policy. For an analysis that sees Bismarck as a
genius whose clumsy successors could not manage the
inheritance, see Henry Kissinger, "Bismarck, the White
Revolutionary," *Daedalus* (Summer 1968), pp. 888–922.

Imanuel Geiss's *German Foreign Policy, 1871–1914*
(London: Routledge and Kegan Paul, 1976), gives an
excellent survey of the diplomacy of the whole period, although the later sections dealing with the First World War
are too much influenced by the anti-German exaggerations
of the Fischer approach, of which more below. Luigi Albertini's massive study, *The Origins of the War of 1914* (London: Oxford University Press, 1952), has a first chapter
dealing with European diplomacy that focuses primarily on
the situation of Austria-Hungary from 1878 to Bismarck's
fall.

For the economic dimension of Bismarck's foreign and
domestic policies, I have been particularly stimulated by
Hans Rosenberg's "Political and Social Consequences of
the Great Depression of 1873–1896 in Central Europe,"
in James J. Sheehan, ed., *Imperial Germany* (New York:
Watts, 1976), and his larger study, *Grosse Depression und
Bismarckzeit: Wirtschaftsablauf Gesellschaft und Politik
in Mitteleuropa* (Berlin: de Gruyter, 1967). S. B. Saul, *The
Myth of the Great Depression, 1873–1896* (London and
Basingstoke: Macmillan, 1972), takes a learned and usefully skeptical look at the economic basis for describing
the 1873–96 period as a "Great Depression," but without,

in my opinion, undermining seriously the view that the period's economic conditions promoted the consequences for industrial organization and political policy perceived by writers like Rosenberg. Two other useful works are Helmult Böhme's *Deutschlands Weg zur Grossmacht: Studien zum Verhältnis von Wirtschaft und Staat wahrend der Reichsgründungszeit, 1848–1881* (Cologne: Kiepenheuer und Witsch, 1972), and Hans-Ulrich Wehler's *Das deutsche Kaiserreich* (Göttingen: Vandenhoeck & Ruprecht, 1975), a condensed version of *Bismarck und der Imperialismus* (Cologne: Kiepenheuer und Witsch, 1969).

For German diplomacy between Bismarck's fall and Bethmann-Hollweg's chancellorship, I have relied heavily on Albertini (vol. 1), Wehler, and Geiss, all mentioned above. For a general study of Caprivi and his policies, see J. Alden Nichols, *Germany after Bismarck: The Caprivi Era 1890–1894* (New York: Norton, 1968). See also Eckart Kehr, *Battleship Building and Party Politics in Germany 1894–1901* (translated and edited by Pauline R. Anderson and Eugene N. Anderson; Chicago: University of Chicago Press, 1973). For a broad study of tariffs and their significance see Kenneth D. Barkin, *The Controversy over German Industrialization, 1890–1902* (Chicago: University of Chicago Press, 1970).

For relations with Britain, see Raymond Sontag, *Germany and England: Background of Conflict, 1848–1894* (1938) (New York: Norton, 1969), and Eckart Kehr, "Englandhass und Weltpolitik," in *Zeitschrift für Politik*, vol. 17, pp. 500–26. For relations with the United States, see Alfred Vagts, *Deutschland und die Vereinigten Staaten* (New York: Macmillan, 1935).

Max Weber's views can be found in H. H. Gerth and C. W. Mills, eds., *From Max Weber: Essays in Sociology* (New York: Oxford University Press, 1946).

Taylor's views on the belligerence of German economic development are drawn from his *Course of German His-*

tory, op. cit., the most conventionally anti-German of his major writings. The general discussion of the German economy in Chapter 3 is drawn selectively from J. H. Clapham, *The Economic Development of France and Germany, 1815–1914* (4th ed.; Cambridge: Cambridge University Press, 1936); Gustav Stolper, *The German Economy: 1870 to the Present* (rev. and expanded ed.; New York: Harcourt Brace Jovanovich, 1967); and Knut Borchardt, "The Industrial Revolution in Germany, 1700–1914," in Carlo M. Cipolla, ed., *The Fontana Economic History of Europe,* Vol. IV, Pt. 1 (London: Fontana Books, 1973). See also David Landes, *The Unbound Prometheus* (Cambridge: Cambridge University Press, 1969), for the relative character, timing, and velocity of economic development in Western countries, in particular Germany compared with Britain. For the relationships of countercyclical policy to the stage of technological development, I am indebted not only to Rosenberg's essay mentioned above, but also to the detailed comments of my erstwhile colleague, Edward Keeton. Also useful to me for general economic information and analysis has been Gerd Hardach, *The First World War, 1914–1918* (London: Lane, 1977).

For classic sources of what I call the "Leninist" view, see Lenin's *Imperialism, the Highest Stage of Capitalism* (1916), in *V. I. Lenin: Selected Works* (Moscow: Progress Publishers, 1971), pp. 162–263, and Rosa Luxemburg's *The Accumulation of Capital* (1913) (London: Routledge and Kegan Paul, 1963). For classic sources of what I call the "Schumpeter" view, see Thorstein Veblen, *Imperial Germany and the Industrial Revolution* (1915) (Ann Arbor: University of Michigan Press, 1966); Joseph Schumpeter, *Social Classes and Imperialism* (Cleveland World Publishing Company, 1968); and Alexander Gerschenkron, *Bread and Democracy in Germany* (1943) (New York: Fertig, 1966). The two interpretations compared and analyzed in Chapter 6 are inspired by Kenneth

D. Barkin's *Controversy over German Industrialization,* op. cit., and Eckart Kehr's *Battleship Building and Party Politics* op. cit. Both works relate various economic interests to party politics and government policies, as well as discuss the Imperial German political and cultural climate. Both are rich and provocative. For the reasons developed in the text, I prefer Kehr's more comprehensive view.

The analysis of German policy leading to the First World War began as a comparison of Luigi Albertini's *The Origins of the War of 1914* with Fritz Fischer's *Germany's Aims in the First World War* (New York: Norton, 1967) and *The War of Illusions* (New York: Norton, 1975). Albertini's work, full of shrewd insight, balance, and passion, is diplomatic history at its very best. Of Fischer, more below. Sidney D. Fay, *The Origins of the World War* (2nd ed.; New York: Macmillan, 1930), less hostile to Germany, remains a seminal work.

My analysis of Bethmann-Hollweg's policies also draws heavily from Konrad H. Jarausch, *The Enigmatic Chancellor: Bethmann-Hollweg and the Hubris of Imperial Germany* (New Haven: Yale University Press, 1973) and Egmont Zechlin, "Cabinet versus Economic Warfare in Germany: Policy and Strategy during the Early Months of the First World War," in H. W. Koch, ed., *The Origins of the First World War: Great Power Rivalry and German War Aims* (New York: Taplinger, 1972).

No one who studies the pre–First World War period in Germany can deny the scholarly energy and seminal influence of Fritz Fischer. Fischer's great works prove clearly that Imperial Germany had imperialist ambitions, but they refuse to deal seriously with whether the ambitions were justified by objective circumstances, or by the same general standard of international morality that animated the other powers. Certainly, a look at the war aims of the various Allies hardly confirms the uniqueness of German ambitions. In any event, was it "wrong" for Germany to want to be a world power like Britain? In an age of imperialism, didn't Germany need colonies? Was it "wrong" for Germany to seek a *Mitteleuropa*? By what standard? Were the imperial Germans foolish to feel "encircled"? Would it have been so easy for a more skilled German diplomacy to have "appeased" France, Russia, and Britain? The answers to these questions are hardly self-evident. They are seldom raised in the Fischer school. Similarly with questions about Germany's domestic regime. Although no one can deny that Imperial Germany's political system had anachronistic parts, is it so clear that the political systems of the Western Allies were any less so? A serious comparative study of the political systems of the major European countries in 1914 would not, I expect, confirm the crude dichotomy between representative Western democracy and Central European autocracy. "Atavistic" and militaristic elites were hardly without influence in Britain or France. In any event, expansionist impulses were hardly confined to such "atavistic" groups. Nor is it clear that a "liberal-democratic" Germany would have behaved much differently. Indeed, as I keep noting, the more "advanced" and "modern" sections of German society – like big business and liberal university professors – were generally far more imperialist-minded than the much-maligned Junkers. It can hardly be taken for granted that a Germany where these elements were even more influential would have been less aggressive. But even if Schumpeter's argument about the predominant responsibility of the Junkers is rejected for the classic Marxist indictment of the bourgeoisie, is it clear that even a socialist Germany would have been any less aggressive or felt any less threatened? Kehr, for one, thought not. For him, nearly all political forces, socialist leaders included, were "materialists" addicted to power. Kehr blames Hegel. But, as I argue, power-hungry materialism was hardly a German creation or monopoly, but a general feature of nineteenth-century culture. In summary, the persistent failure to put their own country in a broader international context, along with an apparent relish for claiming a unique Teutonic wickedness, seems the fundamental flaw in the Fischer school, and indeed beyond it. It is a noble fault, but one more beneficial to the German character than either to the study of history or to the moral improvement of Germany's neighbors.

An interesting study of the debate among German historians over the Fischer approach can be found in John A. Moses, *The Politics of Illusion: The Fischer Controversy in German Historiography* (New York: Barnes and Noble, 1975). Moses makes an interesting connection between Fischer's thesis and Brandt's *Ostpolitik*. A masterful survey of alternative theses among German historians of the causes of the First World War can be found in Wolfgang J. Mommsen, "Domestic Factors in German Foreign Policy before 1914", in James J. Sheehan, ed., *Imperial Germany*, op. cit. Mommsen concludes that the causes of war may be found not only in the blunders and miscalculations of governments, but also in the inadequacy of the German, Austro-Hungarian, and Russian governmental structures. Although his conclusion is doubtless unexceptionable, the implication that German or Austrian policies were rooted in domestic inadequacies rather than legitimate interests of national security and economic policy, or that the Eastern powers were markedly different in these respects from Britain and France, does not seem self-evident. Taylor's review, "Fritz Fischer and His School", in the *Journal of Modern History*, vol. 47, no. 1 (1975), is a healthy corrective to the persistent tendency among German historians to overstress the uniqueness of their national inadequacies. So is V. Rothwell's *British War Aims and Peace Diplomacy, 1914–1918* (Oxford: Clarendon, 1971).

Although I have relied on the major authors mentioned above, I should also like to note a number of recent specialized studies, many by former students of the older authors. A good sampling can be found in the *Festschrift* for Fritz Fischer, *Deutschland in der Weltpolitik des 19. und 20. Jahrhunderts* (Düsseldorf: Bertelsmann Universitätsverlag, 1973), edited by two of his former students Emmanuel Geiss and Bernd Jurgen Wendt. Among others are Horst Müller-Link, *Industrialisierung und Aussenpolitik*, (Göttingen: Vandenhoeck & Ruprecht, 1977); Barbara Vogel, *Deutsche Russlandpolitik: Das Scheitern der deutschen Weltpolitik unter Bülow, 1900–1906* (Gütersloh: Bertelsmann Universitätsverlag, 1973); Volker R. Berghahn, *Der Tirpitz-Plan: Genesis und Verfall einer innenpolitischen Krisenstrategie unter Wilhelm II* (Düsseldorf: Droste, 1971), and "Zu den Zielen des deutschen Flottenbau unter Wilhelm II," in *Historische Zeitschrift*, vol. 210, no. 1 (1970), pp. 34–100; Ekkehard Böhm, *Uberseehandel und Flottenbau: Hanseatische Kaufmannschaft und deutsche Seerüstung* (Gütersloh: Bertelsmann Universitätsverlag, 1972); and Manfred Messerschmidt, *Militär und Politik in der Bismarckzeit und im Wilhelminschen Deutschland* (Darmstadt: Wissenschaftliche Buchgesellschaft, 1975).

Hitler

Hitler's views about Germany's geopolitical situation are constructed mainly out of the following direct sources and collections of conversations and speeches: *Mein Kampf* (Boston: Houghton Mifflin, 1943); *Hitler's Secret Book* (New York: Grove Press, 1961); *The Testament of Adolf Hitler*, François Genoud, ed. (London: Cassel, 1961), which contains a brilliant introduction by H. R. Trevor-Roper; *Hitler's Table Talk 1941–1944* (London: Weidenfeld and Nicolson, 1973); and Hermann Rauschning, *The Voice of Destruction* (New York: Putnam, 1940). Hitler was unusual in the clarity with which he posed his geopolitical options, and the consistency with which he carried each to its logical conclusion. His main ideas were set forth with remarkable consistency in the books written before he came to power, in various recorded conversations with his personal entourage, and in his *Testament*. Yet, Hitler obviously shifted his ideas somewhat from time to time, and certainly was in the habit of telling various audiences what they wanted to hear. This is most apparent in his diplomatic conversations, as can be seen from Andreas Hillgruber's magisterial compendium, *Staatsmänner und Diplomaten bei Hitler: Vertrauliche Aufzeichnungen über Unterredungen mit Vertretern des Auslandes, 1939–1941* (Frankfurt a. M.: Bernard & Graefe Verlag für Wehrwesen, 1967).

An excellent early book on Hitler's career is Alan Bullock, *Hitler, A Study in Tyranny* (New York: Harper & Row, 1962). Hundreds of more recent books and articles deal with Hitler's career and personality. I have consulted extensively Joachim C. Fest's *Hitler* (New York: Harcourt Brace Jovanovich, 1974), which provides a comprehensive and balanced view that incorporates much of the voluminous Hitler scholarship. Fest, incidentally, leans toward the general thesis that Hitler was more Austrian than German. For a study of Hitler's racial ideas and policies, see Norman Rich, *Hitler's War Aims*, 2 vols. (New York: Norton, 1973 and 1975).

A broad study of the prewar Nazi economy can be found in Stolper's general history, *The German Economy: 1870 to the Present*, op. cit. I am also much indebted to Francis Rome for his analysis of Hitler's prewar economy; see his Ph.D. dissertation for the Johns Hopkins University School of Advanced International Studies, "The German National Socialist Regime: Its Response to the World Economic Crisis, Its Ideas and Pre-War Economic Policies."

Hjalmar Schacht's *Confessions of "The Old Wizard"* (Boston: Houghton Mifflin, 1956) is interesting, although obviously self-serving. For authors inclined to stress the evils of autarchy, see Paul Einzig, *Bloodless Invasion:*

German Economic Penetration into the Danubian States and the Balkans (London: Duckworth, 1938 and 1939), and F. C. Child, *The Theory and Practice of Exchange Control in Germany: A Study of Monopolistic Exploitation in International Markets* (The Hague: M. Nijhoff, 1958).

The relationship of the Nazi prewar economy and rearmament is treated in Burton H. Klein, *Germany's Economic Preparations for War* (Cambridge, Mass.: Harvard University Press, 1959); Louis Lochner, *Tycoons and Tyrants: German Industry from Hitler to Adenauer* (Chicago: Regnery, 1954); and Telford Taylor, *Sword and Swastika* (New York: Simon and Schuster, 1959). See also Albert Speer, *Inside the Third Reich* (New York: Macmillan, 1970).

For the significance of blitzkrieg as a way of resolving competing economic and strategic demands, see Burton H. Klein, op. cit. For conservative reactions against Hitler by erstwhile supporters, see Schacht, op cit. and Rauschning, *Voice of Destruction* and *The Revolution of Nihilism: Warning to the West* (New York: Longmans, Green, 1939).

For the organization of the wartime European economy, and notions within the German bureaucracy about how a German-dominated postwar European economy might be organized, as well as Hitler's continuing preoccupation with *Ostraum*, see Jean Freymond, *Le troisième Reich et la réorganisation économique de l'Europe 1940–1942: Origines et projets* (Leiden: Sijthoff, 1974). For an excellent general study, see Alan S. Milward, *War, Economy and Society, 1939–1945* (London: Lane, 1977).

For the large issues involved in appeasement, see Taylor's classic *Origins of the Second World War*. For an analysis of Hitler's policies, see also Klaus Hildebrand, *The Foreign Policy of the Third Reich* (Berkeley: University of California Press, 1973). I am much indebted to my former colleagues at the School of Advanced International Studies: Robert Skidelsky, whose views can be found in "Going to War with Germany," *Encounter,* vol. 39, no. 1 (July, 1972), pp. 56–65; and Kendall Myers, "A Rationale for Appeasement: A Study of British Efforts to Conciliate Germany in the 1930's" (unpublished Ph.D. thesis, Johns Hopkins University School of Advanced International Studies, 1972). Various aspects of the appeasement question from the British side are dealt with in the doctoral dissertations of two of my former students, Simon Newman and Benjamin M. Rowland. As mentioned in the text, Newman's dissertation, dealing with the diplomatic, military, and economic aspects of Chamberlain's Balkan and Polish policy, has become a book, *March 1939: The British Guarantee to Poland* (Oxford: Clarendon, 1976). For a contrasting view, see Sidney Aster, *1939: the Making of the Second World War* (New York: Simon and Schuster, 1973). Rowland's study, which notes Chamberlain's fears of American economic and political power, is summarized in part in "Preparing the Ascendancy: The Transfer of Economic Power from Britain to the United States 1935–1944," in Benjamin M. Rowland, ed., *Balance of Power or Hegemony: The Interwar Monetary System* (New York: New York University Press for the Lehrman Institute, 1976).

Postwar Germany

General descriptions of the postwar German situation are found in Wolfram Hanrieder, *The Stable Crisis: Two Decades of German Foreign Policy* (New York: Harper & Row, 1970); Alfred Grosser, *Germany in Our Time: A Political History of the Postwar Years* (New York: Praeger, 1973); and Paul Noack, *Deutsche Aussenpolitik seit 1945* (Stuttgart: Verlag W. Kohlhammer, 1972). Noack provides an excellent German bibliography for the period. Among those discussing formulas for reunification are Philip Windsor, *German Reunification* (London: Elek Books,

1969); Gerald Freund, *Germany Between Two Worlds* (New York: Harcourt Brace Jovanovich, 1961); Wolfgang W. Schütz, *Rethinking German Policy* (New York: Praeger, 1967); and Ferenc Vali, *The Quest for a United Germany* (Baltimore: John Hopkins University Press, 1967). George Kennan's proposals for a unified neutral Germany are analyzed by Roger Morgan, *The United States and West Germany, 1945–1973* (Oxford: Oxford University Press, 1974). Notable studies in German include Hans Apel, *Spaltung* (Berlin: Voltaire Verlag, 1966); Peter Bender, *Offensive Entspannung: Möglichkeit für Deutschland* (Cologne: Kiepenheuer und Witsch, 1964); and Eberhard Schultz, *An Ulbricht führt kein Weg mehr vorbei* (Hamburg: Hoffmann und Campe, 1967).

For studies of German developments in the Cold War era, see, in addition to several of the above: Harold Zink, *The United States in Germany, 1944–1955* (Princeton: Van Nostrand, 1957); Hans-Georg Schweppenhauser, *Die Teilung Deutschlands als soziale Herausforderung* (Freiburg: Verlag die Kommenden, 1967); Heinrich Siegler, *Wiedervereinigung und Sicherheit in Deutschland* (Hamburg: Rowohlt, 1959); and A. Weiss-Hartmann, *Geschichte der deutschen Spaltung, 1945–1955* (Cologne: Pahl-Rugenstein, 1975).

American and Soviet views on German reunification are analyzed in John Gimbel, *The American Occupation of Germany* (Stanford, Calif.: Stanford University Press, 1960), and Gerhard Wettig, *Entmilitarisierung und Wiederbewaffnung in Deutschland, 1943–1955* (Munich: Oldenbourg, 1967). See also Hans-Peter Schwarz's study, *Vom Reich zur Bundesrepublik: Deutschland in Widerstreit der aussenpolitischen Konzeptionen in den Jahren der Besatzungsherrschaft, 1945–1949* (Berlin and Neuwied: Luchterhand, 1966).

For pointing out to me the differences between Adenauer and Erhard over the Common Market, and their significance for my analysis, I must thank Hans-Peter Schwarz. For sources and analysis, see Konrad Adenauer, *Erinnerungen 1955–1959* (Stuttgart: Deutsche Verlagsanstalt, 1967); Leon Lindberg, *The Political Dynamics of European Economic Integration* (Stanford, Calif.: Stanford University Press, 1963), pp. 125 ff.; and Hans-Peter Schwarz, "Das aussenpolitische Konzept Konrad Adenauers" in *Konrad Adenauer: Seine Deutschland- und Aussenpolitik, 1945–1963* (Munich: Deutscher Taschenbuch Verlag, 1975).

For a further discussion of my views on de Gaulle's policies and various German reactions, see my *Atlantic Fantasy* (Baltimore: John Hopkins University Press, 1970). See also Karl Kaiser, *German Foreign Policy in Transition: Bonn between East and West* (London: Oxford University Press, 1963); and Alfred Grosser, "France and Germany: Divergent Outlooks," *Foreign Affairs* (October, 1965), pp. 26–36. For a definitive French statement, see the unsigned article, "Faut-il réformer l'Alliance Atlantique?" *Politique Etrangère*, no. 3 (1965), pp. 230–44. For a rather critical assessment of de Gaulle's German policy, see Wladyslaw W. Kulski, *De Gaulle and the World: The Foreign Policy of the Fifth French Republic* (Syracuse, N.Y.: Syracuse University Press, 1966). See also Heinz Kuby, *Provokation Europa: die Bedingungen seines politischen Überlebens* (Cologne: Kiepenheuer und Witsch, 1965); and G. Martino, "Die Europäische Union und die Atlantische Verteidigung", in K. Neunzeither, ed., *Die politische Union* (Cologne: Westdeutscher Verlag, 1965).

For Brandt's *Ostpolitik*, see Boris Meissner, *Die deutsche Ostpolitik, 1961–1970* (Cologne: Verlag Wissenschaft und Politik, 1970). See also Willy Brandt, *A Peace Policy for Europe* (New York: Holt, Rinehart and Winston, 1969); and Walter F. Hahn, "West Germany's Ostpolitik: the Grand Design of Egon Bahr," *Orbis*, vol.

16, no. 4 (Winter, 1973), pp. 859–81. Other interesting studies include Arnulf Baring, "Die Wurzeln der Bonner Ostpolitik," *Europäische Rundschau*, no. 4 (1974), pp. 59–75; Louis J. Mensonides, "Bonn's Ostpolitik," in Louis J. Mensonides and James A. Kuhlman, eds., *The Future of Interbloc Relations in Europe* (New York: Praeger, 1974); and Lawrence L. Whetten, *Germany's Ostpolitik: Relations between the Federal Republic and the Warsaw Pact* (London: Royal Institute of International Affairs and Oxford University Press, 1974).

For additional discussions of West German diplomatic options, see Hans-Dietrich Genscher, "Dimensionen deutscher Aussenpolitik heute," *Aussenpolitik*, no. 4, (1974), pp. 363–75; Willy Brandt, "Germany's *Westpolitik*," *Foreign Affairs* (April, 1972), pp. 416–27; W. W. Kulski, op, cit.; F. Roy Willis, *Germany and the New Europe* (Stanford, Calif.: Stanford University Press, 1968); Ralf Dahrendorf, "Themen die Keiner nennt," *Die Zeit*, 24 September, 1976; Hans-Peter Schwarz, "The Roles of the Federal Republic in the Community of States," in Karl Kaiser and Roger Morgan, eds. *Britain and West Germany* (London: Royal Institute of International Affairs and Oxford University Press, 1971), pp. 219–59. See also Schwarz's "Das atlantische Sicherheitssystem in einer Ära ohne grosse Alternativen," in Karl Kaiser and Hans-Peter Schwarz, eds., *Amerika und Westeuropa* (Stuttgart and Zürich: Belser Verlag, 1977).

Formulations of what have been West Germany's principal goals, options, and preoccupations in foreign policy naturally vary by author. Schwarz, for example, sees West German policy as having to reconcile *Deutschlandpolitik, Sicherheitspolitik, Westeuropapolitik*, and *Wirtschaftspolitik* as well as the competing pressures of the U.S.S.R., United States, France, and Britain. Dahrendorf is perhaps closest to my own Atlantic-European-national formulation, although most analyses at least imply this broad categorization. Most agree on Germany's diffidence before definitive choices. Brandt gives a good summary analysis in his *Foreign Affairs* article.

For details of the Helsinki agreement, see *Europa Archiv*, Folge 17 (1975) pp. 437–84. For German views, see H. Abosch, "Helsinki – eine Etappe," in *Frankfurter Hefte*, no. 9 (1975), pp. 2–4; K. Blech, "Die KSZE als Schritt im Entspannungsprozess: Bemerkungen zu allgemeinen Aspekten der Konferenz," *Europa Archiv*, no. 22 (1975), pp. 681–82, and "Die Prinzipienerklärung der KSZE Schlussakte," *Europa Archiv*, no. 8 (1976), pp. 271–5. For subsequent disillusionment with Helsinki, see S. Korbonski, "The Helsinki Agreement and Self-Determination," *Strategic Review* (Summer 1976), pp. 48–58; and Marion Gräfin Dönhoff, "Die Absurdeste aller Grenzen," *Die Zeit*, 18 December, 1976, p. 1.

For various extended analyses of the postwar political-economic system and its troubles, see David P. Calleo and Benjamin M. Rowland, *America and the World Political Economy* (Bloomington: Indiana University Press, 1973), and David P. Calleo, ed., *Money and the Coming World Order* (New York: New York University Press for the Lehrman Institute, 1976). For this view applied to the energy crisis, see my article, "The European Coalition in a Fragmenting World," *Foreign Affairs* (October 1975), pp. 98–112. For a German view, see R. Hertl, "Steht die westliche Welt vor einer neuen Rezession?" *Die Zeit*, 22 November, 1976, p. 7; and Karl Kaiser, "Die Auswirkungen der Energiekrise auf die westliche Allianz," *Europa Archiv*, no. 24 (1974), pp. 813–24.

Various European views expressing dissatisfaction with the present world economic arrangements and suggesting strong protectionist remedies can be found in J. Huntzinger, "Die aussenpolitischen Konzeptionen der Sozialistischen Partei Frankreichs," *Europa Archiv*, no. 12 (1975), pp. 393–04; Robert Skidelsky, "Where Import

Controls Come In," *New Statesman*, 22 October, 1976, pp. 542–3; H. Timmermann, "Die italienischen Kommunisten und ihre aussenpolitische Konzeption: Ein Jugoslawien des Westens?" *Europa Archiv*, no. 21 (1971), pp. 751–60. For an example of European determination to regain national economic control, see Michel Rocard, "French Socialism and Europe," *Foreign Affairs* (April 1977), pp. 554–60.

On the prospects of "bigemony," see C. Fred Bergsten, "The United States and the Federal Republic: The Imperative of Economic Bigemony," in *United States–German Economic Survey 1975* (published by the German–American Chamber of Commerce), pp. 22–7, and "Die amerikanische Europapolitik angesichts der Stagnation des Gemeinsamen Markets: Ein Plädoyer für Konzentration auf die Bundersrepublik," *Europa Archiv*, no. 4 (1974), pp. 115–22. For a critical examination, see Peter Katzenstein, "Die Stellung der Bundesrepublik Deutschland in der amerikanischen Aussenpolitik: Drehscheibe, Anker oder Makler?" *Europa Archiv*, no. 11 (1976), pp. 347–57. For Chancellor Schmidt's disavowal of ambitions or prospects for a Bonn–Washington axis, see, for example, *Der Spiegel*, 6 January, 1975, p. 33.

For gloomy views of Europe, see Henry Kissinger's speech in Pittsburgh, *Department of State Bulletin*, 11 November, 1975, and his television interview with Barbara Walters, reprinted in *Department of State Bulletin*, 5–8 May, 1975. See also Fritz Stern, "End of the Post-war Era," *Commentary* (April 1974), pp. 27–35; Walter Laqueur, "After the Appeasement of the Sheiks: The Idea of Europe Runs Out of Gas," *New York Times Magazine*, 20 January, 1974; and A. P. Whitaker, "The American Idea and the Western Hemisphere: Yesterday, Today and Tomorrow," *Orbis*, vol. 20, no. 1 (1976).

For speculations on Germany's weight within a Soviet hegemony, see Helmut Schmidt, *The Balance of Power*

(London: Kimber, 1969) and Thomas W. Wolfe, *Soviet Power and Europe* (Baltimore: Johns Hopkins University Press, 1970).

For detailed analyses of Germany's postwar reconstruction, see Henry Wallich, *The Mainsprings of the German Revival* (New Haven, Conn.: Yale University Press, 1955); Herbert Mayer, *German Recovery and the Marshall Plan, 1948–1952* (New York: Atlantic Forum Edition, 1969); and Percy Bidwell, ed., *Germany's Contribution to European Economic Life* (Paris: Rivière, 1949).

For the economy in the later postwar years, see Frank Vogl, *German Business after the Economic Miracle* (New York: Wiley, 1973).

For the effects of the oil crisis on Germany, see Horst Mendershausen, *Coping with the Oil Crisis: French and German Experiences* (Baltimore: Johns Hopkins University Press, 1976).

For discussions of declining German productivity, see the OECD *Economic Outlook*, no. 20 (1976), p. 54; the OECD *Economic Survey*, May 1976, p. 45, and *U.S.–German Economic Survey, 1976* (New York: German–American Chamber of Commerce, 1976). The analysis of German economic fears in the late sixties is derived from a variety of interviews and private studies as well as the usual official German, U.S., and OECD sources. For particularly stimulating analyses of current economic conditions, see Kurt Richebächer's newsletters, "Currencies and Credit Markets," sent out from the Dresdner Bank in Frankfurt.

Social Explanations

The bibliography on this topic is endless. I will mention only those books that have directly provoked my own views. Thorstein Veblen presents the germ of the whole school in *Imperial Germany and the Industrial Revolution*

(New York: Macmillan, 1915). Schumpeter's theories are in *Social Classes and Imperialism*, op cit. These are refined and adapted in Alexander Gerschenkron, *Bread and Democracy in Germany*, op cit.

An excellent version of the whole approach can be found in Kenneth D. Barkin, *The Controversy over German Industrialization*, op cit. Barrington Moore, Jr., develops the theory more broadly in *Social Origins of Dictatorship and Democracy: Lord and Peasant in the Making of the Modern World* (Boston: Beacon Press, 1966). Arno Mayer will, I believe, apply certain aspects of it to modern European history in a forthcoming study of the causes of war, portions of which he has been kind enough to share with others in the Lehrman Institute. Eckart Kehr's analysis is in *Battleship Building and Party Politics*, op cit.

For a discussion of the Junkers in the army, see Gordon A. Craig, *The Politics of the Prussian Army, 1640–1945* (New York: Oxford University Press, 1964). For anti-Semitism in the army, see Werner T. Angress, "Prussia's Army and the Jewish Reserve Officer Controversy before World War I," in James J. Sheehan, ed., *Imperial Germany*, op cit. Max Weber's imperialist views can be found in Gerth and Mills, eds., *From Max Weber: Essays in Sociology*, op cit. Nietzsche's aesthetic voluntarism is, for me, most clearly expressed in *Beyond Good and Evil* (New York: Macmillan, 1907). For an interesting view of Nietzsche's influence on German policy in the First World War, and Imperial Germany's general lack of *mesure*, see Charles de Gaulle, *La discorde chez l'ennemi* (Paris: Berger-Levrault, 1944).

Of the innumerable general treatments of Nazi anti-Semitism, I find Hannah Arendt's *The Origins of Totalitarianism* (new ed.; New York: Harcourt Brace Jovanovich, 1966) still the most comprehensive and insightful. See also her bitterly controversial *Eichmann in Jerusalem: A Report on the Banality of Evil* (London: Faber and Faber, 1963).

The text makes clear my debt to Fritz Stern's *Gold and Iron: Bismarck, Bleichröder and the Building of the German Empire* (New York: Knopf, 1977), a moving book, full of information and insight about Imperial Germany. Not the least of its virtues is that its richness of detail and sensitivity of interpretation provide the reader with ample material for drawing conclusions at variance with the author's. See also Stern's *The Failure of Illiberalism: Essays on the Political Culture of Modern Germany* (New York: Knopf, 1972).

For a lengthy analysis of the ideas of the conservative-agrarian economists Adolf Wagner, Karl Oldenberg, and Max Sering, see Barkin, op cit. For an analysis of the role of the agrarians in the maneuvering that led to Weimar's collapse and Hitler's accession, as well as a discussion of the agrarian influence earlier, see Dieter Gessner, "Agrarian Protectionism in the Weimar Republic," *Journal of Contemporary History*, vol. 12, no. 4 (October 1977).

The books that I quote as examples of the "liberal critique" at the outset of the section on "Idealism" in chapter 6 are Karl Dietrich Bracher, *Das deutsche Dilemma* (Munich: Piper, 1971), translated by Richard Barry as *The German Dilemma: The Theories of Political Emancipation* (London: Weidenfeld and Nicolson, 1974); and Ralf Dahrendorf, *Gesellschaft und Demokratie in Deutschland* (Munich: Piper, 1965) translated as *Society and Democracy in Germany* (Garden City, N.Y.: Doubleday, 1967). Both Bracher and Dahrendorf are prolific writers and I do not claim to have exhausted their ideas. Dahrendorf, in particular, seems to be evolving rather in the direction of my own critique. See, for example, his article, "Baader-Meinhoff – How Come? What's Next?" in the *New York Times*, 20 October, 1977, p. 23.

The best exposition and defense of the Idealist position in English to my knowledge is Bernard Bosanquet, *The Philosophical Theory of the State* (1899) (New York: Macmillan, 1958). I have attempted to come to grips with this tradition in my *Coleridge and the Idea of the Modern State* (New Haven, Conn.; Yale University Press, 1966). For my earlier attempt to analyze the philosophical underpinnings of de Gaulle's politics, see also my *Europe's Future: The Grand Alternatives* (New York: Horizon Press, 1965).

Index

233